Daily Fragrance of the
Lotus Flower

Daily Fragrance of the Lotus Flower

Ji Kwang Dae Poep Sa Nim

Volume 1
1992

Bo Duk Religious Research Center
Mountain View, Hawai'i

Energy Spiritual Writing Paintings by Ji Kwang Dae Poep Sa Nim.

Front cover: "Helping for Your Wishes to Come True. Attaining Buddhahood." *Acrylic on canvas.*

Back cover: "Bodhisattva Protecting the Globe, Bringing Peace and Great Prosperity." *Acrylic on canvas.*

First Published in 2011
by Bo Duk Religious Research Center
P. O. Box 787
Mountain View, HI 96771 USA

© 2011 Ji Kwang Dae Poep Sa Nim
ISBN: 978-1-936843-00-8
ISSN: 2159-0869

All rights reserved. No part of this book may be reproduced or transmitted in any form or by any means, electronic or mechanical, including photocopying and recording, or in any information storage or retrieval system, without prior written permission from the publishers.

Author's Opening

Dear Reader,
In the clear, crisp night sky each individual star shines brightly, adorning the heavens with its beauty. The radiance of each star encompasses the whole world and brings forth a beautiful mind for anyone whose gaze takes in the brilliance of the stars, making that person and everyone else happy.

It is just like this: each person is also like one of the bright, shining stars in the beautiful night sky. Without any stars, there is little beauty in the night sky, and the sky itself loses much of its value.

Each individual person is as important as each shining star that gives beauty to all sentient beings. Each person that eliminates his or her impurities by practicing sincerely will become clearer and brighter and ever more radiant. Each practicing person will become like a bright, shining star in the dark sky.

Since July 17, 1992, without missing a single day, through Buddha's message I have been writing the Daily Sutras to help bring out the wisdom that is within each and every one of us.

Each teaching is like a simple reminder that helps you throughout the daily ups and downs of your busy lives, so that in the end you can become like a bright, shining star.

All of the teachings fit the energy of the particular day they are written. Yet, as you read the teachings gathered here, you will see that each and every one of them is actually timeless. These always timely teachings help you by offering beautifully simple ways of understanding and grasping the perplexity of our daily lives as we deal with others, in friendships, in love relationships, in our work, and in pursuing self realization.

As you read these teachings you will see that they are not only for students of Buddhism. They can be applied by anyone, regardless of background, religion, age or gender.

I hope that you enjoy reading these teachings and become your own bright shining star.

Ji Kwang Dae Peop Sa Nim

Foreword

The Daily Fragrance of the Lotus Flower is a comprehensive collection of the daily teachings that have been offered by Ji Kwang Dae Poep Sa Nim, the Supreme Matriarch of the Yun Hwa Denomination of World Social Buddhism, since July 17, 1992. Divided into yearly volumes, this collection is a treasure-store of daily life wisdom. Each teaching is, in truth, a "daily sutra" authored by Ji Kwang Dae Poep Sa Nim in enlightening response to the life issues and questions of Her students and to the shifting complexion of local, national and world events. Whereas the teachings of the historical Buddha — Siddhārtha Gautama or Shakyamuni Buddha — were memorized by His students and passed down orally for generations before being committed to writing, the daily teachings of Ji Kwang Dae Poep Sa Nim have been written by Her own hand, each and every morning, in immediate response to the energy and issues of the day.

This is the first of a precious series of yearly volumes of *The Daily Fragrance of the Lotus Flower* that will be published in an ongoing fashion. Each of the teachings in each volume expresses both the means-to and the meaning-of unblemished clarity and unhindered compassion. As daily sutras, these teachings at once demonstrate enlightened engagement with the relational dynamics of daily life and offer directly useful methods for realizing that there are ultimately no impediments to transforming every situation into the bodhimandala, or "place of enlightenment." Respectfully received and mindfully read, the teachings collected in these volumes are an illumination from within of our ever-changing human situation — a revelation of the suchness (tathātā) of daily life and the incomparable and unending path of appreciative and contributory virtuosity.

Social Buddhism

Social Buddhism is the Dharma (Teaching) of daily life wisdom. Social Buddhism is not above sentient beings, and it is not below sentient beings; it is within and together with sentient beings in order to eliminate ignorance and to attain and skillfully enact wisdom.

The origin of Social Buddhism dates back to the time of Shakyamuni Buddha. The Buddha's recorded teachings (Pali: *suttas*; Sanskrit: *sutras*) reveal the Buddha interacting with and providing wise and compassionate guidance to people from all levels of society — from manual laborers to royalty — in meadows, on mountain peaks, in parks, private homes and palaces. All of these teachings take the form of conversations between the Buddha, his disciples, both ordained and lay students, and people living in the villages, towns and cities that he visited. Most often, the teachings begin with the Buddha being asked a question emerging from the daily life experiences of those fortunate enough to meet him. Thus, from its very beginnings, Buddhism has been socially engaged. Today, Social Buddhism is most thoroughly exemplified by the teachings and practices of the Supreme Matriarch Ji Kwang Dae Poep Sa Nim of the Yun Hwa Denomination of World Social Buddhism. This volume and those to follow collect the Daily Sutras offered by Ji Kwang Dae Poep Sa Nim to Her students and to the rest of the world. They are a treasure house of contemporary daily life wisdom.

Social Buddhism is Omniscient Buddhism and the most encompassing form of Buddhism, embracing teachings and practices from Theravada, Mahayana, Vajrayana and Zen Buddhist traditions. As in other forms of Buddhism, Social Buddhism joins monks and nuns and laypersons through the teachings of Buddha (which means 'the absolute,' 'the truth'), the study of *suttas* or *sutras*, meditation practice, and (as in Zen) the formal teaching of koans (Korean: *kongan*; Chinese: *gongan*). In Social Buddhism, one has to know and honor both the Dharma taught by the Buddha, and the ethical precepts (Vinaya) that inform the Buddhist community (Sangha). But one must also know and honor the customs and manners appropriate in each place and at each time. First and foremost, however, Social Buddhism teaches the means-to and the meaning-of living a correct life every single day, exemplifying a correct mind moment-by-moment.

What distinguishes Social Buddhism from other forms of Buddhism is that the Social Buddhist doctrine is so direct, pure and true (encompassing) that it is able to improvise fluently with the patterns and dynamics of contemporary life, while resolutely guiding people onto the path of Buddha. Unlike traditions that have come to be tightly bound up with specific cultural norms and constrained by fixed paradigms and dogmas rigidly adhered to for centuries, Social Buddhism is flexible enough to respond to people's minds as they have come to be through each person's individual karma, all while following the original Dharma of Shakyamuni Buddha.

In order to have a correct life, one must follow three kinds of practice.

1. Keeping the precepts.
2. Having a meditation mind and dwelling in quietude.
3. Attaining wisdom in order to eliminate ignorance.

If one does not keep the precepts, one's mind becomes hindered and bothered, making it difficult for one to be clear. When one's mind is not in quietude, it is constantly undulating, also rendering one unclear. Finally, dissolving ignorance — the root of trouble and suffering — requires wisdom. That is why these three categories of practice are so important. They are the foundation of Social Buddhism.

While Shakyamuni Buddha was alive, Buddhism most commonly took the form of an ascetic practice reserved for monks and nuns. During the first three-month retreat after Shakyamuni Buddha's *parinirvana* (ultimate release), his students held a Council to recite collectively all the teachings of the Buddha remembered by those present. Roughly 100 years later, a second Council was held to establish a comprehensive canon of the Buddha's teachings. About a half-century later (in the middle of the third century BCE), as a result of disputes about the Vinaya, or rules for monks and nuns, different denominations of Buddhism began to appear.

Mahayana Buddhism began to emerge as a distinct set of teachings and practices about 100 years later in the second century BCE. Over this same period of time, what is now known as Theravada also became established as a distinct tradition. As in the Buddha's original Sangha, Mahayana Buddhism was taught to everyone, regardless of their social status, but still followed the strict ascetic practices associated with Theravada Buddhism. Also, whereas the

Theravada accorded great respect to the *arahants,* or students of the Buddha who realized the meaning of Buddhist practice and liberation, the Mahayana offered greatest reverence to *bodhisattvas,* or beings who dedicate themselves to skillfully-assisting all sentient beings in the realization of liberation.

Although the peoples of Korea may have long had contact with Buddhism through the Silk Roads trade that linked India, Central Asia and East Asia, Mahayana Buddhism was formally introduced to Korea from China by an imperial mission sent during the Korean Goguryeo Dynasty in 372. Buddhism was quickly embraced in Goguryeo and the other kingdoms that existed during the same period on the Korean peninsula, Baekje and Silla. During the Three Kingdoms period, in addition to the Chinese imperial mission that sent Buddhist texts and images to Korea, Korean masters were also traveling to China, bringing back Buddhist teachings.

Buddhism was first formally adopted as a state religion in 529, when the king of Silla officially embraced Buddhism. A court noble named Ichadon was to be executed because of his Buddhist faith. He informed his executioner that to believe in Buddha is the truth, and that as proof of this, white blood would spill from his body once they carried out his execution. White blood did flow from Ichadon's body, and King Beopheung (514–540) was so impressed that he decided to make Buddhism the official state religion of Silla in 529.

From Korea, Buddhism spread to other parts of East Asia, and by the 7th century was well established throughout the region. During the Unified Silla Dynasty, two great masters Uisang (625–702) and Wonhyo (617–686) traveled to Tang Dynasty China and officially brought key Buddhist teachings back to Korea, including the Flower Ornament or Avatamsaka Sutra. Uisang founded the Wonyung (Hwa-eom; Chinese, Huayan) School that has been the foundation for Korean Buddhist doctrinal traditions to the present day. Wonhyo sought to synthesize various Buddhist teachings in an all-inclusive vision and to combine these with Buddhist practices that were effective in daily life as well as in monastic settings.

Bodhidharma, who was the twenty-eighth patriarch in India, exemplified the third form of Buddhism which came to be known as Chan (in China), Zen (in Japan) or Seon (in Korea). Bodhidharma lived during the fifth century. From South India, Bodhidharma traveled to China to see King Wu of the Liang Dynasty (Yan Mun Che) and began to teach Buddhism there, becoming known thereafter as the first patriarch of Chan Buddhism. Before Bodhidharma's arrival, the Chinese studied and practiced various traditions of Mahayana Buddhism, and especially emphasized carrying out bodhisattva actions and building up virtue. King Yan Mu Che was very happy that a great master like Bodhidharma would arrive from India. The king told Bodhidharma that he built many temples, funded Buddhist translation work and did many bodhisattva actions. The king wanted to know how much virtue he had created through all these actions. Bodhidharma told him that he made "no virtue." The king was infuriated and told Bodhidharma, "You said that my virtue is nothing, but you are supposed to be a great master and the twenty-eighth Patriarch. In fact, who are you?" Bodhidharma told the king, "I am nothing." The king did not understand this profound response and the true teaching Bodhidharma was offering to him. Instead, the king only had murderous thoughts, and Bodhidharma left the southeastern coast of China and traveled north to Mount Song (or Sorim Mountain) near the Chinese capital of Luoyang. There he meditated for nine years without once touching the wall with his back to show the value of the practice and the meaning of Zen. Bodhidharma's teaching centered on realizing the one true nature of all things, understanding karma and practicing mindfulness in all situations.

Bodhidharma did not seek students, but one young man named Hea Ga (Huiko) is said to have cut off his arm in the snow to show how much he wanted to learn from Bodhidharma. Bodhidharma decided to teach him, and Hae Ga went on to become recognized as the second patriarch of Zen Buddhism in China. Bodhidharma's lineage became prominent in China with the sixth patriarch, Huineng, who focused on realizing one's own true nature and demonstrating sudden enlightenment or readiness for awakening (*dunwu*). The Chan tradition developed many branches, but enlightened masters like Baizhang, Huangbo, Mazu and Linji came to figure in all the lineages transmitted into Korea and Japan. Chan (Japanese: Zen; Korean: Seon) Buddhism centers on meditation and a special mind-to-mind transmission, beyond words and letters; but Chan also respected the history of Buddhism, attainment of the truth of the sutras and the importance of an enlightened teacher in realizing one's true self. According to Chan, if one does not have clear teaching and guidance, one can easily fall into debilitating vacuity.

Buddhism in Korea went through its most difficult time during the Yi Dynasty (Joseon) (1392–1910), because the dynasty's founder,

King Yi Seong Gye (1335–1408), adopted Confucianism and demoted Buddhism from its position as the national religion. During the earlier Goryeo Dynasty (918–1392), temples were located in villages and were a central part of everyday life. It was not until the Yi Dynasty that temples were forced to move into the mountains. Confucianism existed during the Goryeo Dynasty, but it was not officially recognized as a state religion as in the Joseon.

A key moment for Social Buddhism occurred when the great master Dae Gak Guksa (Uicheon), who was the fourth son of Goryeo Emperor Munjong, traveled to China during the Song Dynasty (1086). Dae Gak Guksa returned from China as a strong advocate of the Cheontae (Chinese: Tiantai; Japanese: Tendai) School, which had adopted the Lotus Sutra as its central scripture. On his return, he established the Cheontae Denomination as a distinct tradition. Cheontae, which quickly became a major, syncretic force in Korean Buddhism, combined an emphasis on meditation (central to Seon/Chan/Zen) and non-duality (central to Hwa-eom/Huayan). It later branched out into several other denominations. Among these new branches was the Poep Hwa Denomination.

Supreme Matriarch Ji Kwang Dae Poep Sa Nim was a student of the Poep Hwa Denomination and eventually received the title of archbishop. Soon thereafter, the Supreme Patriarch of the Poep Hwa Denomination handed down the lineage and Patriarch Kim Gap Yol gave Ji Kwang Dae Poep Sa Nim the title of Supreme Matriarch.

When Supreme Matriarch Ji Kwang Dae Poep Sa Nim came to the West (first to the United States of America and then to Europe), She brought not only the lineage of Cheontae Poep Hwa:

through Her attainment, She realized that global conditions were opportune for revitalizing Shakyamuni Buddha's method of daily teaching in the context of everyday life and for a new flowering of His unbroken lineage of Social Buddhism. To symbolize this, Supreme Matriarch Ji Kwang Dae Poep Sa Nim decided to change the name of Her Cheontae Poep Hwa denomination to Yun Hwa or Lotus Flower. While Poep Hwa means Dharma Flower, the original symbol of Buddhism is the blossoming of the lotus. Supreme Matriarch Ji Kwang Dae Poep Sa Nim is the first Matriarch of the Yun Hwa Denomination of World Social Buddhism.

Social Buddhism has existed since the time of Shakyamuni Buddha. Although Shakyamuni Buddha wanted to teach Social Buddhism, he had to respond to the people living during that period and the quality of their thoughts and mindfulness. Because of their ideologies and concepts, Shakyamuni Buddha had to stress a stricter and more ascetic teaching and practice. Similarly, when Dae Poep Sa Nim first began accepting students in Honolulu, they just wanted good luck and ceremonies, but were not really interested in learning the Dharma. It was not until later, in 1984, when Dae Poep Sa Nim traveled to Europe, that She found students who were open to learning the true Dharma.

During the time of Shakyamuni Buddha, one of His lay students, Vimalakirti, taught a form of Social Buddhism, and Shakyamuni Buddha was very appreciative of that. Shakyamuni Buddha even sent Moon Soo Bodhisattva (Manjusri), the bodhisattva of awareness and wisdom, to attend Vimalakirti. But even Vimalakirti was not able to develop Social Buddhism to its full extent because the mind of the people was inclined more toward ascetic practice.

Social Buddhism is unique in providing the daily life wisdom to perform one's correct function and duties as a human being while also attaining enlightenment. Without going into the mountains and living apart from society, one can live one's daily life and yet also be able to see oneself and reflect upon oneself correctly. One can realize the highest levels of attainment in the very midst of the social world through cultivating true and clear relationships. Social Buddhism is truly boundless.

Supreme Matriarch Ji Kwang Dae Poep Sa Nim is recognized by many to be one of the few masters since Shakyamuni Buddha who has dared to teach and demonstrate what Social Buddhism is by being a living exemplar.

For example, until now, masters and particularly patriarchs or matriarchs always have had to wear formal Dharma robes as part of the Buddhist tradition. The traditional clothing worn by matriarchs and patriarchs is used to show their status and to insure that they receive the proper respect for their attainment. But when Supreme Matriarch Ji Kwang Dae Poep Sa Nim came to Europe, She wore the traditional clothing of a master when She was teaching, but also went beyond the tradition and wore layperson's clothes. Bringing to life the teaching of Chan Master Linji that Buddhist realization means being a "true person of no-rank," Supreme Matriarch Ji Kwang Dae Poep Sa Nim thus demonstrated the bodhisattva meaning of according with every situation and responding as needed. Moment by moment, simply and directly, Her teaching is tirelessly translating the true meaning of Social Buddhism into virtuosic action.

Because of Her great enlightenment, Supreme Matriarch Ji Kwang Dae Poep Sa Nim makes no disparaging differentiations or discriminations among religions or beliefs; everybody and everything is the same, and is part of one world and one universe. This is a truth that has been proclaimed throughout humanity. Social Buddhism teaches that activating the truth of non-duality is realizing that all beings are the same, precisely because they can differ-from and differ-for one another. Through mutual contribution and appreciation, this very situation can become a living paradise.

Secretary Monks
Lotus Buddhist Monastery

Daily Fragrance of the Lotus Flower

Volume 1
1992

"What I am teaching you is not new. You heard about it before in either this or a past life. This daily teaching is simply to remind us so that we can be clear and live correctly in this and future lives. Believing this teaching is entirely the decision of the one who reads it. In addition, applying one's own concept to this teaching is the choice of the reader himself or herself."

— *Ji Kwang Dae Poep Sa Nim*

1. July 17, 1992. Honolulu
Have a fortitudinous mind, be a trustful person, and when there is a secret, keep it.

To keep secrets means to forget everything; do not hold them in your memory.

2. July 18, 1992. Honolulu
Always try to speak correctly and do not say things which hurt others. Unnecessary speech always bothers oneself, just like a dog who bites his own tail and suffers from it.

When you can forget about making both good and bad speech, then you can make correct speech.

3. July 19, 1992. Honolulu
When wise persons receive love, care and protection from their master, friends or others, they become more humble and attain greater thankfulness. For such persons, the path of enlightenment is very near.

When ignorant persons receive love, care and protection from their master, friends or others, they become more arrogant. Such people think that they are very important and that that is why they received such treatment. For them, the path of enlightenment is far away.

4. July 19, 1992. Honolulu

The Buddha path is very lonely and desolate. But if you enjoy and become friends with loneliness and desolation, that is the path to become a Buddha.

Being lonely and desolate means you do not bother others or show them who you are. Enjoying and becoming friends with loneliness and desolation means that you always keep a thankful mind.

5. July 20, 1992. Honolulu

When you are in loneliness and desolation, go one step further inside of them. Then you can see your true self and see that until now all of your desires and the things that you wanted were nothing but the devil's play and game.

6. July 21, 1992. Honolulu

The practice person should not be afraid of other human beings.

The person who gives me the most difficult time is the person who wakes me up.

The person who is sycophantic towards me shows and helps me to realize how much greed I have.

Do not be afraid of any human being and be thankful to them all.

7. July 22, 1992. Honolulu

Suffering mind and happy mind are not two. But when you are suffering you forget about happy mind and when you are happy you forget about suffering mind.

But the practice person always polishes his or her mind without making discriminations, and attains and enjoys every moment.

8. July 23, 1992. Honolulu

Before you met the practice, your path was not clear; it is for that reason that you were wandering around, suffering.

But the practicing person's path is always clear. Once you are on this path, do not give rise to doubts; just go vigorously ahead.

As you practice, whatever doubts appear are your karma and devils. So whatever it is, follow the present situation and go ahead like a bulldozer.

9. July 24, 1992. Honolulu

This world is burning like a fire, but do not try to escape from it.

Enjoy it, and at the same time extinguish your own fires, one by one. This is the way to reach the Buddha path.

10. July 24, 1992. Honolulu

When a duty is given to you, do it yourself.

If out of your laziness and ego you pass it on to someone else, though your body may feel comfortable in that moment, you gradually denigrate yourself and nobody will welcome you anymore.

11. July 25, 1992. Honolulu

Always watch the greed and desire appearing in your each moment. Do not fall into and drown in them.

Always perceive where your greed and desire are coming from. 1, 2, 3...

12. July 25, 1992. Honolulu

See yourself today. How much did you do good things for others and how much did you bother others? Perceive your actions.

See how much you spoke truthfully today and how much you spoke dishonestly. Perceive your speech.

practice harder *infinite happiness*

13. July 26, 1992. Honolulu

Love others before you try to win them over. Forgive others before you blame them. At the same time, see and repent for your karma.

P. S. Everything occurs and appears as a result of what you did before.

14. July 27, 1992. Honolulu

Strategy of the Mouth

Always watch your speech which is coming out from your mouth. Is it bothering others or is it making others happy?

An insecure person's speech always bothers others. A secure person's speech always makes others happy.

But the person on the Buddha (absolute) path uses the eyes rather than the mouth.

15. July 28, 1992. Honolulu

The happiest people in the world are those who empty themselves of desire, greed and conditions, living only for others and to make them happy.

Also, when people have someone to love and because of that are able to empty out all greed, desire and conditions, they are the happiest people in the world.

16. July 29, 1992. Honolulu

The mind is Buddha. The body is sentient being.

The practice person does not follow what is appearing from the body, such as sensations, feelings, greed, lust, desires, anger, and the 84,000 delusions.

Always remember that the mind is Buddha, and make this body a Buddha, too.

17. July 30, 1992. Honolulu

The more you use a bronze bowl, the shinier it becomes. It is the same with our bodies: the more you use them, the healthier they become.

All body sicknesses come from laziness. So wherever you are and whatever you do, always work diligently.

However, always relax the mind and let it become lazier and lazier, until it cannot even move.

18. July 31, 1992. Honolulu

I see the moon.

I want to know the moon.

I want to have the moon.

I want to go into the moon and I want to become one with
the moon.

This is the Buddha path. Always practice vigorously and have endurance and patience. If you cannot get it this life, there is always next life.

("Moon" is truth, absolute, love and great enlightenment.)

19. August 1, 1992. Honolulu

To go into Buddha's world (which means the absolute, clarity and truth), there are always many obstacles. To eliminate these obstacles is the purpose of practice.

Look into your actions and what you have done today. How much of the time were you angry and how much of the time did you remain patient? See that, and then throw everything away. If there is even a tiny thing left, that tiny thing will become your karma.

20. August 2, 1992. Honolulu

True leaders, politicians, teachers, doctors, etc., do not look at others, and do not think about someone else's mistakes. Only look into yourself and see what your mistakes are.

People who can really see themselves will know what enlightenment is; those who realize what their own mistakes are will be able to truly help others.

When someone who can truly help others is among even myriads of millions of people, he or she can always stay in and enjoy tranquility.

21. August 3, 1992. Honolulu

True feeling is when you do not feel it. That moment is just comfortable, and the mind becomes like that of a child. That is true feeling.

True love is when you and I become one and I forget about myself. The person who thinks about himself does not yet know what love is.

22. August 3, 1992. Honolulu

$$1 + 1 = 0$$
The person who attained the truth
$$1 + 1 = 1$$
The practice person
$$1 + 1 = 2$$
The non-practice person

23. August 4, 1992. Honolulu

Be a needed person for others. But when others want you, do not become arrogant.

When you are not a needed person for others, you are like a broken bowl.

When others want you, be happy about it and do 100 percent for them. This is the true path of happiness.

24. August 5, 1992. Honolulu

As one's path gets deeper, a wise person becomes humbler and knows how to thank his master or teacher.

As one's path gets deeper, an ignorant person becomes haughty. That person is like a wild tiger biting the hand of the master who feeds him.

Humility builds one's virtue. Haughtiness pushes one into the devil's world and eternal suffering.

25. August 5, 1992. Honolulu

$$1 + 1 = o$$
$$o + o = O$$

('1 + 1' means 'I, my, me'; '=' means 'practice'; the small 'o's mean 'truth'; and the large 'o' means 'Buddha' and 'supernatural penetration power'.)

26. August 6, 1992. Honolulu

Absolute love rain always wets all the trees.

But because some trees are shaded and do not receive the rain, they always suffer. The shade is the karma that they have built up.

So practice vigorously and come out of the shade.

27. August 6, 1992. Honolulu

To Remove the Shade

There are no trees without roots. But when human beings do not know their roots, they wander and suffer.

Human being's roots are their parents, siblings, master or teacher, and friends. So first respect and be filial to your parents; second, care for and love your brothers and sisters; third, always be thankful to your master or teacher; and fourth, stay close with your friends.

Whoever understands these points and puts them into action will always receive lots of love from others.

28. August 7, 1992. Honolulu
To Eliminate an Inferiority Complex
The person who does not have confidence in himself is always afraid of everything and is caught by his past.

When you know what your past mistakes were, never try to cover them up. Instead, make an effort to fix them.

The way to fix your past mistakes is to make others happy in this moment. But when you make others happy, forget about it and remember,

$$1 + 1 = 0$$

(Inferiority complexes come from relationship karma.)

29. August 8, 1992. Honolulu
Today's Poem
   Darling, in your bright, shining, cozy and snuggly embrace,
   I will always live a beautiful life;
   I will make beautiful thoughts, speech and actions.
   And in your embrace,
   I will make that place brighter and more beautiful.
   I will help others to not dirty that place,

And will help them to not make suffering for you.
And Darling, I will definitely make your embrace
Even softer, cozier, brighter and more beautiful.
GOSH! You make me feel so good!
KISS!!!

30. August 8, 1992. Honolulu
(is a cartoon—see originals)

31. August 9, 1992. Honolulu
The True Taste of Life
When the flower has fully blossomed and the leaves are verdant, you indulge in yourself and you do not know the true taste of life.

When the flower and leaves fall and all that remains is the bare stem, then you finally get to know the true taste of life.

However, practice people can always enjoy the true taste of life. Only, when you are healthy like the blossomed flower, do not become arrogant; and when you are like the naked stem, do not become weak.

32. August 9, 1992. Honolulu
Do not make a separation between social life and spiritual practice life. Wherever you go, whatever you do, always keep the practice mind, and no matter how difficult others are, do not get caught by them. Always engage others with the practice mind.

In the beginning, even if you receive derision and scorn from others, keep a fortitudinous practice mind.

No matter how difficult others are, as time goes by they will follow the practice person. The reason is that all human beings have the spiritual mind, but the opportunity for them to practice did not arrive yet.

33. August 10, 1992. Honolulu

What is the significance of the shit that was on Shakyamuni Buddha's head during his time of practice? It means that any kind of attack or anything which comes from outside is not a hindrance and that all devils which appear from inside are eliminated, one by one.

Do not make a difference between inside and outside; only make tranquility. And do not give rise to thinking about the dirtiness of the shit. Instead, perceive what the thing is which makes the shit dirty, and at the same time go one more step inside of there.

34. August 10, 1992. Honolulu

This whole world is one family.

Absolutely no difference between human beings. It is just like throwing the same seed over a wide area: the only difference is the place where the seeds land and germinate. That is why all human beings are one family.

Let us realize this as soon as possible and eliminate fighting and warring within our one family. And dear practice persons, let us practice vigorously, attain the truth of life, and make this world beautiful and an infinite paradise, as soon as possible.

35. August 11, 1992. Honolulu

I always make myself. When I make myself happy, all becomes happy, and when I make myself sad, all becomes sad.

When I make myself greedy, a catastrophe follows. When I make myself humble, virtue follows.

Always watch this 'I', and see what it is. And keep practicing.

36. August 11, 1992. Honolulu

When you make a mistake, do not pull others into the situation. Instead, repent for your mistake so that you do not do it again.

When you bring others into it, the size of that mistake becomes twice as large.

37. August 12, 1992. Honolulu

If you want someone to trust you, you must first trust Buddha (absolute energy and truth).

If you want someone to respect you, you must first respect the master or teacher, and others.

Trusting mind eliminates one's karma, and respecting mind makes one become a great master and Buddha in the future.

38. August 12, 1992. Honolulu

Today's Poem

    The sound of the waves soars.
    That sound comes to the ears and is so glorious.
    Blue waves undulating,
    Not knowing where they are going.

Throw this body into the waves
And clean it of all past, present and future karma.
Offer everything to my beloved darling and go together.
Do not ask where we are going.
On the path of going with my beloved darling,
I do not have to know where we are going.
La, la, la, la!!
One step, two step…

39. August 13, 1992. Honolulu

Ancestor's Day, August 13, 1992
Dear respected ancestors,

Today, cut off all the bad karma you created before in this world. With Buddha's love, compassion and exquisite power, please stay in peace and comfort, in heaven.

When you are reborn into this world, please become a bodhisattva and a Buddha, and help and teach all ignorant sentient beings. Make this saha world a Buddha-land (absolute and true land) and adorn it with infinite beauty.

40. August 13, 1992. Honolulu

All suffering and troubled sentient beings, do not get caught by trouble and suffering. Caught by them, your suffering only increases.

Remember that behind suffering, bright, wide and absolute happiness always awaits you. Always remind yourself of this and wash away your suffering and trouble.

Also, when you think that you have already washed away your suffering and trouble, do not become proud and arrogant. Treat the trouble and suffering you had as your teachers, continue practicing, and become a bodhisattva who can help wash away the trouble and suffering of others.

41. August 14, 1992. Honolulu
Letter to Buddha, Absolute Energy, Truth
I always miss you so much and I want to be in your arms perpetually. In this morning's dream I was in your arms, in your warm and majestic embrace. There, I forgot everything. I wish to abide there eternally.

42. August 15, 1992. Honolulu
This whole world is just like a mirror. Always see your reflection in the mirror and see what you are. Do not indulge in your outside form.

Perceive your own life. Today, am I receiving respect from others? Or, because of my desire, am I bothering others? Or, because of my sadness, am I making others sad?

Always look into yourself and if something is not correct, fix it. You cannot hide or escape from this mirror. Even if you hide in a rat hole, this mirror will always reflect what you are, so do not try to escape.

Until you can see your clean reflection, polish yourself and practice.

43. August 15, 1992. Honolulu

In this moment, what is in your mind? Express that honestly.

44. August 16, 1992. Honolulu

One wishes that others are happy. But then, when someone else becomes happy, even though one congratulates him, one's mind does not want to congratulate that person.

One promises oneself to help others. But then, when someone else becomes better than oneself, one's mind turns angry.

One expresses one's love for others. But then one's mind turns hateful.

Because one wants to keep one's status and position, one's mind turns sycophantic.

The practice person strives continuously to put these 1, 2, 3 minds into one place.

But always remember, behind these 1, 2, 3 minds there is no-mind.

$$1+, 2+, 3+ = 0$$

45. August 17, 1992. Honolulu

True independence means always to have a mind of repentance. Even if you have the tiniest thing that bothers others or the tiniest thing that hates others, these will become your chains and enslave you; they are the cause of dependency suffering.

Repentance means to cleanse yourself and to go into Buddha's bright and clear path. In the bright and clear path, the *teakll* always makes effect. The *teakll* which hates and bothers others is the cause of suffering, and the *teakll* which loves and helps others is the cause of happiness.

So always repent for your mistakes, become bright and clear, make a bodhisattva *teakll* and attain true independence.

46. August 17, 1992. Honolulu
(is a cartoon—see originals)

47. August 18, 1992. Honolulu
Do not be moved by slander and do not be moved by praise.

Being slandered is the medicine through which one realizes oneself; being praised is the chance to look into oneself again.

A dog always indulges in the meat thrown to him. But a keen-eyed lion bites the person who threw the meat.

Practice people, always be clear and bright and do not be hindered anywhere. Become a liberated person and go ahead, one step, one step...today and tomorrow.

48. August 18, 1992. Honolulu
When you know how to tame the angry lion just like a child, you can really attain true happiness.

The angry lion is this world's situation; true happiness is the path of practice.

49. August 19, 1992. Honolulu

There is no place in which the dharma does not exist. Sentient beings live in the dharma.

Dharma is not only in the temple. Keeping the dharma even while outside temple is the true path, because in the midst of social life one's desire and wanting mind can easily lead to forgetting the dharma.

The successful person always keeps the dharma and the precepts while being in the social life.

The true temple must be inside of one's mind.

50. August 20, 1992. Honolulu

Life gift from Dae Poep Sa Nim: *The Essence of 84,000 Sutras and 2,500 Years of Enlightened Masters' Teaching*

- love + love = love
- hate + hate = hate
- hate + love = delusion
- love + hate = desire
- practice + practice = great love, great compassion, become Buddha

51. August 20, 1992. Honolulu

Sentient beings are always in the bright and clear Buddha-land and all seeds come from there. When a bad seed appears, a bad thing grows. The seed means karma.

The practice person is not hindered by good or bad seeds. Always practice, polish yourself and find sentient beings' original place. In the original place, just live a right life.

A good seed + a bad seed = right life: "Hi! I'm here. What may I do for you?"

(Note: the "=" sign means practice)

① + ① = ②

① + ① = ①

① + ① = ○

○ + ○ = ○

52. August 21, 1992. Honolulu

Just because you know this o, do not become arrogant or complacent.

The mind which says, "I know," is sentient beings' mind; the mind which says, "I do not want to know," is also sentient beings' mind.

Do not make "know" or "don't know" mind. To really attain this o (absolute mind), concentrate on your daily life and practice regularly. That is really attaining this o place and making it bright and shining.

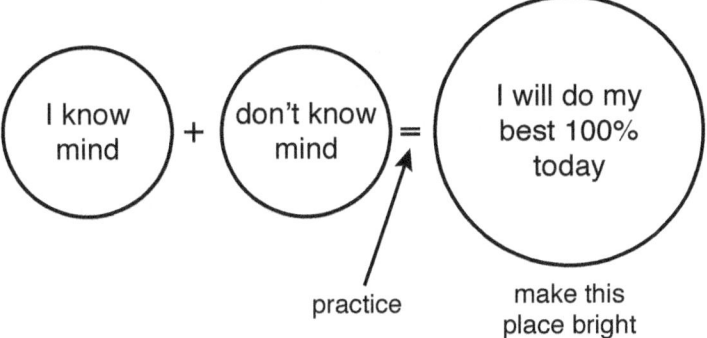

53. August 22, 1992. Honolulu

Every day or every morning when you go into the social world you can easily forget about your clean, true self. While immersed in the social whirlpool, you can easily make the same karma as others.

But the practice person always watches his eyes, watches his mouth, watches his ears and watches his nose.

Whenever and wherever you go, do not make unnecessary karma; try to understand people who bother and hate you, and practice for them. And remember,

$$1 + 2 = 0$$

("1 + 2" is the social world, and "=" is practice, which makes 0 and which will make the correct function of 1 + 2 = 3.)

But always remember,

$$1 + 2 = 0$$

54. August 23, 1992. Honolulu

The beauty of nature, the glory of nature and the exquisiteness of nature are just like us human beings.

Everything comes from complete quiescence. This is the law of the universe.

Always practice, polish yourself and go into complete quiescence. And when you break and come out from quiescence, make beautiful speech, action and thought, adorning this world just like nature's beauty.

$$1 + 1 = 0$$
$$0 + 0 = \textit{(drawing of dove; see original)}$$

55. August 24, 1992. Honolulu

True relation comes from 0: a relation that has already been in the 0.

When 0 was dirty, they did not know each other.

When 0 becomes clear and bright, true relation appears and has a beautiful effect on life: the supernatural power of 0 and the exquisiteness of 0.

Dear practitioner, always practice and polish 0; find the true self; meet the true lover and live life without any hindrance.

$$0 + 0 = \textit{(drawing of two happy hearts; see original)}$$

1 + 1 = *(drawing of one, partially darkened heart; see original)*

56. August 24, 1992. Honolulu

That face of yours which makes all delusions disappear is like a Buddha's face in the Dharma room.

That face of yours which makes a pure and innocent smile is like a baby Buddha.

That face of yours which is so happy that it forgets everything is like a butterfly sitting comfortably and peacefully upon a flower.

When I am in your arms, all 84,000 delusions disappear: this becomes Buddha's place.

Sharing this happiness with all others makes them happy and makes this world become the Pure Buddha Land, adorned with true beauty.

57. August 24, 1992. Honolulu

True love and true beauty are flowers that bloom on an old, dead tree.

Despite thunder and storms, that tree stands gloriously. Then one morning, a flower blooms, making others happy.

Endurance and practice are the Buddha's path, just like flowers blooming on an old dead tree.

Keep practicing; everything will be accomplished.

58. August 25, 1992. Honolulu

A long time yearning to see a true lover from far away; then one morning, that lover is before your bright and shining eyes.

Do not try to find the Buddha from far away. When you try to find Buddha from far away, that is seeking nothing but fantasy and delusion. Always watch in front of you; find your true jewel in the very near.

When you cannot see this jewel, it is because it is covered by the six senses and your own karma. Always polish yourself and practice this. Become a Buddha's bright eye, cut off this world's five desires and understand others' situations.

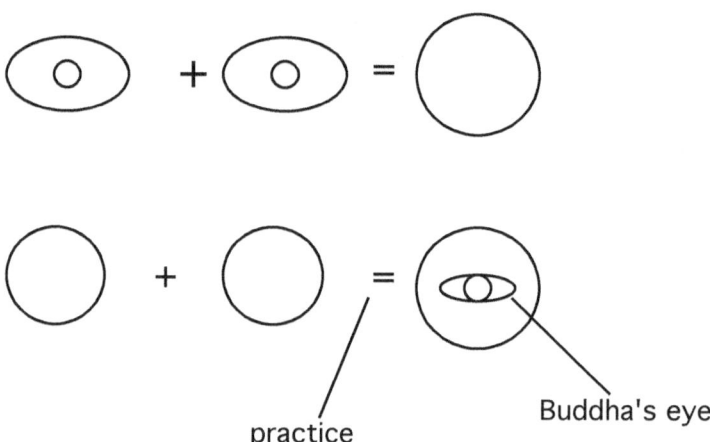

59. August 25, 1992. Honolulu

There is one pure and clear thing which appears and disappears in the bright and clear place.

Do not attach to what appears. Do not lament what disappears.

Always keep brightness and clarity.

When it appears, let it appear beautifully. When it disappears, let it disappear beautifully.

Beauty makes Buddha; ugliness makes sentient beings.

$$1 + 1/2 + 1 + 1/2 = \bullet$$

$$1 + \text{🪷} + 1 + \text{🪷} = \bigcirc$$

60. August 26, 1992. Honolulu

A beautiful relationship is when the mind is completely relaxed and tranquil. When you are completely relaxed and tranquil, you can meet the correct partner. When you are completely relaxed and tranquil, you meet the true partner. When, after meeting the true partner, you remain tranquil and relaxed, that is true love. Living in tranquility and relaxation, that love will last eternally.

Always relax, be tranquil, practice vigorously and make beautiful love.

The lotus flower looks more beautiful and brilliant when it is in the calm and tranquil pond.

61. August 27, 1992. Honolulu

The person who has a clear goal is the most successful and happy person.

The path to accomplishing your goal has many obstacles. But always continue going toward your goal, even if it is difficult, and even if you suffer. Always go into that path.

It is the same with the bodhisattva's vow. To keep the vow is not easy, but when you keep your vow and go in that direction, that is the path of achieving Buddhahood. As you keep your vow and go into that direction, your suffering and obstacles become your own formula for teaching others.

Dear practitioner, do not neglect or take your vows lightly. The vow of one's true self is to keep one's true self. To keep your true self and others' true self is the most glorious thing. Please, always keep your vow and go into this path step by step, every day.

While you keep your vow and go into that path, lotus flowers will appear in your tracks and make others happy. But when you neglect your vows and take them lightly, the five desires and eight sufferings appear in your tracks. That path makes you and others suffer.

$$\text{VOW} + \text{VOW} \underset{\text{practice}}{=} \bigcirc$$

$$\text{5 Desires} + \text{8 Sufferings} \underset{\text{neglect}}{=} \text{Path of Suffering Sentient Beings}$$

62. August 28, 1992. Honolulu

Do not get caught by karma. Karma sometimes makes one become a Buddha and sometimes makes one become a devil. It is always confusing oneself and hurting others.

Do not get entangled by karma. Always watch the karmic games going on around you and perceive your own karma. Become a master of your karma and treat it like your servant.

All sentient beings who are suffering in karma, please find your bright, clear and true master as soon as possible and govern your karma in a beautiful way. That is the Buddha path.

63. August 28, 1992. Honolulu

1. Always love and be faithful to Buddha.
2. Always love and be faithful to the master who teaches you.
3. Always be a loving and faithful husband to your wife.
4. Always be a loving and faithful wife to your husband.
5. Always be loving and faithful to your parents.
6. Always be loving and faithful to your children.
7. Always be loving and faithful to your friends and become a trusted friend.
8. Always be loving and trusting to your country and become a faithful and loyal citizen.
9. Always be loving and faithful to the whole universe and become a holy person.
10. Always love and trust Buddha and become a Buddha yourself.

$$1 + 2 + 3 + 4 + 5 + 6 + 7 + 8 + 9 + 10 = 0$$
$$1 + 2 + 3 + 4 + 5 + 6 + 7 + 8 + 9 + 10 = 55 \text{ KARMA}$$

64. August 29, 1992. Honolulu

Human beings always like holding onto their own world and are always striving to keep their own self and protect their own world so that no one may attack them.

But the worlds human beings hold onto are karma worlds, and the more you try to protect yours, the more you separate yourself from others.

Inside the walls of karma they build up around themselves, people become lonely and suffer from loneliness. Sometimes in the midst of their loneliness, people suddenly meet the lover for whom they were longing. But the happiness that results is only momentary because they are soon attracted again by their own world: how could they be truly HAPPY?

True relationship is breaking the walls of karma you have built around yourself; it means returning to non-self, which means going back to the 'Big I' world. Then you can make a beautiful and true relationship.

Dear practitioner, remember, $1 + 1 = 0$.

In the 0 always make a together, true world. Build a wall of love to be protected from the attack of one another's 'karma I' and adorn this present world with true beauty.

65. August 30, 1992. Honolulu

Hell and heaven are not different. When there is no hell, there is no heaven. 'I' in hell is actually 'I' in heaven. Hell which makes heaven is actually heaven.

Do not be afraid of any situations and circumstances; just go. Enjoy hell as it is and always make heaven and share it with others. Live in infinite heaven.

Hell + Heaven = 0

66. August 30, 1992. Honolulu

One promises oneself for the millionth time to eliminate delusions, desires and ego. But according to the situation, these repeatedly appear. There, one's ego becomes much stiffer and the mind which sees this makes more suffering.

Dear practitioner, do not suffer. Polish that mind which can see this, treat delusions and desires as your lovers, and make ego into a humble friend. Right here, do not escape but find yourself.

This is the path of Buddha

67. August 30, 1992. Honolulu

When I eliminate my 84,000 delusions, ego, and the five desires, I finally find myself. In this moment, I am sitting here as it is, drinking coffee.

The taste of the coffee when I drank in delusion and the taste of the coffee after I found myself, are they the same or different? If you say, "different" it is not correct; and if you say, "the same," it is also not correct.

Which one is correct?

KATZ!

The smell and taste of this morning's coffee are wonderful: I am drinking in the Buddha.

Hello, darling! Please come here and have a cup of coffee. This morning, your shining eyes make me brighter. This place is actually heaven. Thank you very much!

68. August 31, 1992. Honolulu

Always keep this bright and clear place and eliminate the devil which is in the mind; only go to the path of Buddha.

While going to this path, do not hesitate or be afraid of difficulties; only go to the path of Buddha.

Do not be afraid of 84,000 delusions; always go to the path of Buddha.

Do not get caught by sweet or sour tastes; always go to the path of Buddha.

The length of this present life is very short. Do not waste time; always go to the path of Buddha.

Our true life is infinite; always go to the path of Buddha.

Relax comfortably on Buddha's infinite, golden grass until linking to another life: this is the infinite path of happiness.

69. September 1, 1992. Honolulu

In the bright and clear purity there are other bright and clear purities.

The first bright and clear purity is one's true nature. The second bright and clear purity is that which makes one be born into this world. The third bright and clear purity is that which makes one build oneself up.

If you want to be a true human being, first find this bright, clear and pure place and make your true 'I'. Then, in the bright and clear purity, bury all good, bad, comfortable and uncomfortable conditions and delusions. Just go back to nothingness and find the true 'I'.

$$1 + 1 = 0$$
$$2 + 0 = 0$$
$$3 + 0 = 0$$

$$0 + 0 = \left(\text{Buddha 'I' which is true 'I'} \right)$$

70. September 2, 1992. Honolulu

Oh, you! Mystical and shining one,
You are the master of the whole universe.
I have been wandering around many thousands of years,
    trying to find you.
Now I have finally found you. I become one with you; I
    am so overjoyed!
Shall I give it to the sun which is in the sky or to the moon?
    No!
Shall I give it to the sentient beings who are on this globe?
To whom on this globe shall I give it?
Deluded sentient beings still do not see me, and they do
    not even try to find me. How can I give it?

But in the world, there are practicing people. That makes me feel at ease.

Dear practitioner: Can you see? Can you hear? Not yet?

Practice vigorously and this happiness will be yours in the very near future.

71. September 2, 1992. Honolulu

Unconditional you.

Undeluded you.

Desireless you.

Egoless you.

The moment when I am with you, I forget myself: time and space do not govern me anymore.

I am deeply sinking into you, just following the wind and clouds, going anywhere, giving this happiness to others, and living infinitely.

Oh, you! Even if I say, "I love you," that is not correct. Even if I say, "I forgot the love," that is still not correct. What shall I say?

I love you infinitely, infinitely forever. Even if this whole universe disappears and another universe appears, I will still love you infinitely, until atoms break and disappear.

72. September 3, 1992. Honolulu
The True Pollution of the Globe

In this world, there are 5 billion separate minds. These 5 billion separate minds always play separately. In these 5 billion separate minds, there are always 84,000 delusions appearing and disappearing, which cover this world with 420,000 billion rains, thunders, winds and clouds.

In the 5 billion separate minds, the smallest number is when two minds become one mind. At that time, love is being created.

That one love mind which comes from two minds can put 5 billion separate minds into one place and can make one pure mind. Can you see how powerful, how strong and how glorious this mind is?

Dear practitioner: Eliminate all delusions from your mind and realize this theory of two minds becoming one.

Husband's mind becomes one mind with his wife's mind.
Wife's mind becomes one mind with her husband's mind.
Friend's mind becomes one mind with his friend's mind.
Parents' minds become one mind with their children's minds.
Children's minds become one mind with their parents' minds.
Leader's mind becomes one mind with the citizens' minds.
Citizens' minds becomes one mind with the leader's mind.
Monks' and nuns' minds become one mind with the precepts and their master's mind.

Everyone, become one Buddha mind, live without fears, and live in eternal happiness.

73. September 4, 1992. Honolulu

Practice Vigorously

Everything can be accomplished by practice. The path of practice is our way of truth and is the way to build up our true self.

The relations that appear through the practice life are true relations, and the love which appears through the practice life is true love.

Human beings come from within karma. If we let ourselves go according to karma, everything becomes impermanent and we become disappointed and very unhappy. The lives of those human beings who let themselves go according to karma are full of suffering; they do not yet know what true happiness is.

But the path of practice teaches us what real happiness is, leads us to the realization of it, and allows us to do the correct function of human life.

Forget about karma, and think and remember:

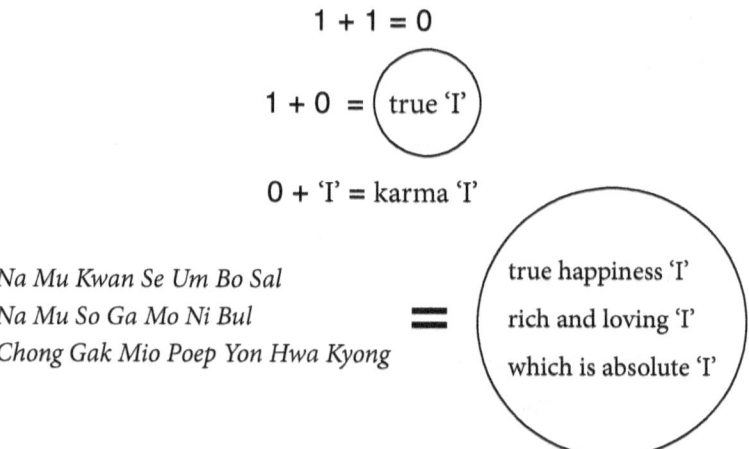

$$1 + 1 = 0$$

$$1 + 0 = \left(\text{true 'I'}\right)$$

$$0 + \text{'I'} = \text{karma 'I'}$$

Na Mu Kwan Se Um Bo Sal
Na Mu So Ga Mo Ni Bul   =   (true happiness 'I'
Chong Gak Mio Poep Yon Hwa Kyong   rich and loving 'I'
                                    which is absolute 'I')

74. September 5, 1992. Honolulu

GREAT, BRIGHT, GLORIOUS YOU! I always live in you.

Until now everyone called your name, 'Buddha' or 'God' or 'Truth' or 'Absolute Energy'. One master called you, 'Dry shit on a stick'; another, 'Three pounds of flax'. Some even yelled at you, 'KATZ'!!!

They gave you 100,000 different names, whatever names they wanted to. But how many people knew you truly?

Until now, when they knew you just a little bit, they got transmission. Just by going a little near you, they <u>also</u> got transmission. Those who thought they knew you were the ones who historically discredited you and made you suffer.

GLORIOUS, WONDERFUL YOU, please forgive the egotistical and deluded sentient beings; please love and help them unconditionally. Enable them to realize and make your place bright and clear. Let all sentient beings live in your place and have true, infinite, happy lives.

Na Mu Kwan Se Um Bo Sal
Na Mu So Ga Mo Ni Bul
Chong Gak Mio Poep Yon Hwa Kyong

75. September 6, 1992. Honolulu

The shining, bright and clear master of this whole universe (Buddha, truth, absolute energy) is always bright, strong and faster than a missile. That power can achieve everything and can create anything in this whole universe. It can make the globe revolve, the sun and moon shine, and can make everything grow. That power can especially create human beings.

What is this glorious and shining master's original place? This original place is not devilish, rough, arrogant, stiff or poky. This glorious power always comes from the softest, gentlest, brightest and clearest place.

Those who practice always makes themselves as soft and gentle as possible; this means making soft and gentle speech, action and thought, and realizing that soft and gentle place. Practicing people especially keep soft and gentle love and communication for relationships, and make all relationships soft and gentle. This softness and gentleness is a subtle and exquisite power which cannot be broken by any kind of rough or strong thing.

To go in that direction is the path of Buddha. To go in that direction is to make oneself a Buddha.

76. September 7, 1992. Honolulu

Whoever is caught by greed, desire and lust, and cannot get away from it, will never know the true taste of life. They will not know how to digest the teachings and will put themselves, as well as others, on the path of suffering.

Desires and greed are like a cloud floating in the sky. Do not let yourself go in there; it leads to the path of suffering.

Always look at the bright and clear sky which is behind the clouds. Our truth is like the bright and clear sky. The bright, wide and clear sky is our truth and is our big 'I'. The floating cloud is our desire, greed and lust. Do not waste your time chasing the floating cloud. Always make yourself like the bright and wide sky and live a true life without greed, lust or desire.

Remember, 1 + 1 = 0

77. September 7, 1992. Honolulu

Always be the biggest person. Do not waste energy on small greed and desire; always do big things. Doing big things is the path of finding our true selves and is the path of the infinite.

Do not be a slave to your delusions and desires which appear every day. Be the biggest master so that you may conquer your delusions and desires and command them as you wish.

Your biggest enemy is inside of you, not outside. Conquer all of your devils, become a triumphant person, and live life without any hindrances.

78. September 7, 1992. Honolulu

Do not test the person whom you think you love.

Do not try winning over the person whom you think you love.

Do not act in ways which you think the person whom you love does not like.

Do not bother or make suffer the person whom you think you love.

If you put all of these points into action, that is the path of eliminating one's karma. This path is the way to become a Buddha yourself and is the way to receive love from millions of people. This will enable you to live an infinite, happy and true life with your lover.

Remember: become a no-mind master.

79. September 8, 1992. Honolulu

An enlightened person's mind always has great space.

An unenlightened person's mind does not have space. Whenever and wherever, an enlightened person's mind can fit into any kind of situation. When dealing with children, it becomes a child; when dealing with adults, it becomes an adult; when dealing with a holy person, it becomes a holy person. When an enlightened person meets a bad person, he acts like a bad person, but changes the other person's mind so that he or she becomes a good person.

Enlightened people are just like water without a bowl: they can enter a bowl, assume its shape, and then break the bowl and return to the original water nature. But an unenlightened person is like water that always stays in the same bowl and becomes stale and rotten.

An enlightened person's path is to always break darkness and make everything shine. An unenlightened person's path is to make everything dark, wherever he goes.

Unenlightened people cannot see enlightened people, even if they are right in front of them. Unenlightened people are only attached to their own bowl, so they do not know how to see or respect others. But for enlightened people, it does not matter who they are dealing with; they give respect to everyone and also practice for unenlightened people to become enlightened.

Dear practitioner: realize your true nature as soon as possible; break your own bowl and come out of it. Become quiet, spacious and tranquil water; live life correctly. And whatever situation you encounter, flow without hindrance and do human beings' correct duty.

80. September 9, 1992. Honolulu

Thousands of years spent fighting with 84,000 enemies. But one day, in the early morning dew, everyone capitulates.

Climbing on the back of the mountain, gazing in the four directions—north, south, east and west—the world which was small suddenly becomes bigger and everything becomes wide, bright and clear.

Ah! Because of me, all 84,000 enemies are vanquished. Now, in this moment, the 84,000 witches, devils and enemies become so pitiful. Each enemy suffers greatly because of fighting with me and trying to defeat me. I sincerely apologize for that.

To compensate for your suffering, every day I will practice vigorously and make you joyful, beautiful and happy.

84,000 enemies − 84,000 enemies = 0

0 + 0 = 84,000 happiness

81. September 9, 1992. Honolulu

Comfortably relaxed, easily going inside of the Buddha's bosom in Hawaii.

While sweetly sleeping for a lovely two months, I heard a sound which annoyed me. So I opened my eyes.

The restless baby God (Dong Ja) was trying to wake me. I asked, "What is the matter?"

Suddenly, with a bright smile, the baby God said to me, "Now you are ready to leave."

"Where to?"

"The Buddha in Europe has been waiting for you since last month."

"Then, why didn't you wake me up?" I asked.

"You were sleeping so peacefully, I couldn't wake you."

"Oh! Then I have to go."

"Is your love suitcase ready?" asked the baby God.

"Yes."

"Then let's go."

Why is it that this time when I'm going away everything looks so beautiful? Why is there a sweet scent to it? Ah! The Buddha in Europe planted lots of lotus flower seeds and took care of them. That is why there is a sweet scent. Thank you very much, European Buddha.

Especially today, the clouds in the sky feel so comfortable and look so beautiful.

82. September 10, 1992. Honolulu

Everybody has a beautiful mind inside of them. But inside their beautiful mind there is anguish, fantasy, desire and greed. Because everyone lives inside of their karma, their beautiful minds do not show.

Being born poor or rich is according to one's karma. If one's mind is beautiful, one can be rich; but if one has an ugly mind, one lives in a poor situation. But by practicing strongly, one may eliminate one's anguish and fantasy. Then a beautiful mind appears and one's action, speech and everything becomes beautiful.

The person who has a beautiful mind always gives beautiful things to others and makes beautiful actions. That person may live a rich life, eternally.

The person who presently lives in a poor situation must find a beautiful thing in his mind and use it as soon as possible to eliminate his poor situation and find the answer to how to live a rich life, eternally.

A husband gives beautiful gifts to his wife. That giving mind enables him to find the path to live a rich life, eternally.

83. September 11, 1992. Los Angeles

Behind longing mind, there is no-mind.
Behind loving mind, there is no-mind.
Behind hateful mind, there is no-mind.
Behind jealous mind, there is no-mind.
Behind angry mind, there is no-mind.

Always remember this. Do not attach to or suffer over what appears each moment. Take one more step inward. There, no-mind is waiting for you.

Go into no-mind and turn longing mind into happy mind so that you can meet again soon. Turn loving mind into non-desire mind so that you can give your whole life to your loved ones and have unconditional love. Turn hateful mind into amiable mind. Turn jealous mind into understanding mind. Turn angry mind into embracing mind.

Attain this so that every day you can make anyplace your paradise world.

84. September 12, 1992. Los Angeles

Meeting Buddha (absolute energy, truth, great love) always seems to be so far away and difficult. But one day you suddenly meet Buddha, put everything down and sink into true happiness.

But suddenly, karma calls you and you must leave. In that moment, you feel so forlorn and have such difficulty expressing yourself. It is like being someone who has always lived alone and been very lonely, and then without warning he finally meets the lover for whom he has yearned for so long. They get to know one another and finally two become one. They live so happily, every single day. But each one has his duties to do, and so they must part. They promise to meet again, but once parted, they suffer because they have so much missing mind.

You always want and yearn to be with Buddha. But because of your leftover karma, you always have to leave.

If you wish to always be with Buddha, practice vigorously and eliminate your karma. It is just like when you wish to live with your loved one: you put all of your effort into working hard.

If you practice vigorously, your karma will disappear and you will be able always to live with Buddha. Then you will have infinite happiness, just like two lovers who do not live apart for even one minute. Two become one, and they enjoy infinite happiness.

Do not doubt your practice, just as lovers do not doubt about their love. They give one another unconditional love and have unconditional happiness.

85. September 13, 1992. Paris

When someone is happy, show him a sincere and congratulatory mind. But if you see that someone is happy, and on the outside you congratulate him but inside are jealous, do not become depressed that you are not happy like he is.

Depressed and jealous mind always puts one into unhappiness. Then you cannot go near happiness and you do not know what it is.

Do not forget that someone else's happiness is actually your happiness. Always remember that.

If you really want to be happy, practice vigorously. The more you practice, the shinier you become. Also, when your karma disappears, your happy day will come, absolutely. It is just like when the spring comes, flowers bloom.

But if you want the flowers to bloom in the winter too, keep a true congratulatory mind for others. Discover the flower for which winter is no hindrance.

86. September 13, 1992. Paris

The sound of the seagulls is so piercing and high; the sound of the waves, so loud.

Sitting all alone on Malibu beach, I suddenly appreciate that I am here, in this saha world.

How many sentient beings can really see me?

I push away all the clouds in the four directions and suddenly appear here and see you.

Again I am so astonished and enchanted by the universe's subtle power and by the Buddha's absolute supernatural power; they are so magnificent and glorious.

Without realizing it, I automatically *hapchang* and give my thanks and appreciation to the Buddha.

Dear Buddha: Inside of you, I put my head down and give benediction to all sentient beings so that they can meet you as soon as possible, and within you, live in infinite happiness.

87. September 14, 1992. Paris

You who stand steadfast in the midst of storms, rain and wind, wearing wet clothes, there is a bright thing which shines. Ignorant sentient beings only look at your wet clothes and disparage you. That disparaging mind is sentient beings' mind.

The mind which sees the shining thing inside of the clothes is the mind of Buddha.

In the midst of all kinds of difficulties and irritations, keep oneself and stand steadfast. The mind of vigorous practice is the mind of Buddha.

In the mind of Buddha, there is a colorful, shining, true and priceless jewel. Sentient beings who only attach to wet clothes, how can they discover this priceless jewel?

Kwan Se Um Bo Sal changes clothes all the time according to sentient beings' level and travels around this saha world. Sometimes Kwan Se Um Bo Sal wears wet clothes, sometimes dry clothes, sometimes Dharma robes and sometimes ordinary clothes. How can you see this Kwan Se Um Bo Sal?

Practice people, take off your 'dirty clothes' as soon as possible, attain Buddha's mind, greet Kwan Se Um Bo Sal's honored visit. Become one with Kwan Se Um Bo Sal and beautifully adorn this present world.

Dirty clothes – wet clothes = Kwan Se Um Bo Sal's shining robe
Dirty clothes – Kwan Se Um Bo Sal's shining robe =
the priceless jewel inside of Buddha

88. September 15, 1992. Paris

Always think of Buddha's place, just like you think of your lover.

Always think of the inside of Buddha's place, just as though you have come together with your lover.

Always think about how to adorn and create beauty in this Buddha's place, just as lovers come together and plan how to make a happy life.

To be with Buddha eternally is like living with your lover eternally. To do so, practice vigorously, eliminate your karma and polish yourself.

To be one with your lover: practice and practice, and become Buddha yourself.

89. September 15, 1992. Paris

The love of husbands, wives, boyfriends and girlfriends is just like wearing a warm and weatherproof coat in the winter. With this love, wherever you go you feel very secure and relaxed.

But ignorant and unwise people always hold onto their own conditions, thinking about I, my, me. Because of that, they remove this love coat. And, they are always changing this coat for that coat, each time making their bodies more frail. It is just as though they become naked and suffer in the winter.

But wise people do not abandon the coat, even if it does not fit them well; they alter the coat as they need and wish. Should a coat get old and worn out, they patch it nicely and keep themselves warm and secure.

Men's and women's relationships are coming together as a result of the great connection they have. Husbands and wives, especially: do not doubt your connection. Always be thankful for it and for being together. Regardless of what kind of situation you have, always embrace one another, harmonize, create true, great love, and live happily together.

90. September 16, 1992. Paris

In a corner of the beautiful city of Paris, I saw a beggar shivering. Without realizing it, I halted my footsteps and looked at him. He was a pitiful sight. I opened my handbag, took out some money and gave it to him. He was so happy and thanked me many times.

Unconsciously, I looked at his face very closely. In his shriveled and dirty visage he had the wish to survive. In that moment, I automatically gave him energy. His face lit up and he smiled.

In his smile I saw all of his suffering and karma, and how he has entangled himself in the many mistakes he has made in this life and the last. I saw the difficulty he has freeing himself from his karma.

Especially in his last life, he was very lazy, stole from others and lived solely for his own convenience. He did not like to work and only wanted to play. He also loved to drink, and greatly enjoyed womanizing and giving his ladies a hard time.

As a result, not too long ago in this life, all of his family deserted him. Even now, he continues believing that he is always right and has a very large ego. He has no job and is sick; and so he lives on the street. He is very pitiful.

If this person had encountered practice and had known even just a little about the path of Buddha, all of this misfortune would not have befallen him.

I gave him a benediction so that he can wake from his darkness and someday meet the Dharma. If he cannot do so this life, then he can in the next.

Dear practitioner: please be happy and thankful that you are in the path of Buddha now and that you have this practice life. If you practice vigorously, your life will never become like this man's.

91. September 16, 1992. Paris

Sitting, standing, sleeping, walking, I always think about you. The more I think about you, the more absolute energy flows from my body. I give this energy to all others in order to eliminate their suffering and to make them happy.

Thankful for you, infinite you, for your care, your concern, your guidance, your magnificent comfort and your great love. I am always inside of you and I am so happy; I do not know how to express this happiness.

Great you, I love you infinitely. I live life only for you, life after life.

Hot kiss, kiss, kiss, kiss!!!
("You" means Buddha, absolute, truth, lover.)

92. September 17, 1992. Paris

If there is too much anguish, you cannot sleep.
If there is too much happiness, you cannot sleep.
If there is too much interest, you cannot sleep.
If there is too much anger, you cannot sleep.
If there is too much jealousy, you cannot sleep.

The human body is affected by how we use our minds. That is why Buddha always says to set your mind in the middle, like an ocean among continents, keeping your mind like a tranquil sea.

But it is difficult to keep the mind that way all of the time. Human beings are always living in the midst of suffering, and it becomes a lifelong habit. Because they remain in and know how to take suffering, when complete happiness appears they do not know what to do with it; they find it hard to deal with and govern. It is as though humans are living in a cloud, and when it dissolves, the strong, hot sun is revealed and people do not know how to handle it.

Practice people: in the near future many happy things will appear, and so you must learn how to deal with and govern happiness. You must also strive to make that happiness become true happiness.

The way of practice is to make a path of happiness. So you must learn how to correctly share happiness with others.

Suffering − suffering = happiness
Happiness + happiness = astonishment
Happiness + happiness − happiness = true happiness

93. September 17, 1992. Paris

This present world is like a spider's web. But with your great love we can make a hole in the web, go through it and overcome all difficulties.

No matter how difficult it is, with your great love I always become tranquil and relaxed. This is due to your great protection.

Make true love into a pillow. Then, when I lie on the floor everything becomes so at ease and comfortable and the whole world is mine. What more can I ask for? I can only say, "Thank you" and "love you…."

94. September 18, 1992. Paris

I reflect upon what I shall write on the white sheet of paper. But I automatically draw a lotus flower. My mind becomes bright, clear and beautiful.

It is very strange. Before, on the white sheet of paper I always wrote about my suffering, conditions and delusions. Why now did those things completely disappear? It amazes me.

I am now sitting very comfortably in the lotus flower which I drew, and I put my lips to my warmest lover's hand. Past, present, and future thinking cease. I just become one with my lover. While floating together upon the calm ocean, all the debris around me disappears. It is very interesting.

Ahhh! So this is Buddha's great love and compassion.

Na Mu Kwan Se Um Bo Sal
Na Mu So Ga Mo Ni Bul
Chong Gak Mio Poep Yon Hwa Kyong

95. September 18, 1992. Paris

Light is illuminating my shriveled mind. The light gradually increases and makes this shriveled mind open. The world which I saw until now becomes completely different. What is this?

Suddenly, the wilted flower beside me comes to life, the noise of the car's horn outside becomes melodious, and the voice of the woman who is making a lot of noise in the kitchen sounds like a beautifully played piano. What happened?

Until now, I always imagined what paradise was like. But this is paradise!

My mind is full of light. Where does hell exist? What is this light? Ahh! This light is due to absolute, true love.

I put my lips to the glass of wine and take one sip. The taste suddddrrrrrr in my throat and tingles me. Without realizing it, I smile.

What is the difference between this smile and the smile of Mahakashapa for which he received transmission from the Buddha on Yong San Mountain 2,500 years ago? How are they different?

Smile, smile, smile!

96. September 19, 1992. Paris

Drawing the circle. While drawing the circle, I draw your face inside of it. Your benevolent smile makes me very happy. I put my face to your face, that which I yearn for so much. In that moment, all of my karma and conditions from my last life to this life are purified. I become just you and you become just me.

To your non-doubting mind I give myself and everything and make the inside of this circle shine and shine and live together with you, eternally.

Shining you, love you eternally.

○ + ○ = ☼

97. September 19, 1992. Paris

As your position becomes higher and more important, always lower yourself more.

If you try to show off when your position becomes higher, misfortune will appear; the position that was given to you will lose its luster, and you will cause others to suffer.

Remember, the riper the rice plant is, the more its head bends down.

When you are together with your lover, be attentive to your lover and do your best for that person. The mind which is attentive to one's lover is the bodhisattva mind and whoever has that mind will be infinitely free and will have an eternal love life.

98. September 19, 1992. Paris

Dreams always seem to be connected to the present time and they affect many situations. But do not lose yourself in dreams and do not attach to them; you must come out of the dream.

Just because you had a bad dream, do not let yourself worry all day long. If you had a bad dream but you think positively, the bad dream can change and take a positive direction and can become better than what you had expected.

Dreams are often connected to one's karma. So always try to eliminate your karma and do not be hindered by any dreams. Do not attach to anything, and go to the bright and clear place.

If you have bad dreams, practice harder, see your karma, and eliminate it. And remember, every day is a good day.

99. September 19, 1992. Paris

If you want someone to love you, always polish yourself. And if someone does not know what love is, teach him.

True love is to always lower yourself and raise others.

But if the person who you raised becomes arrogant and acts recklessly, do not fight about it. In that moment, give him a compassionate smile and leave his place. Going away creates space to help that person realize his mistakes.

Make others as a Buddha.

The path of making others as Buddhas means to first polish yourself. Then, once you begin shining, others automatically become Buddhas.

Always remember,

1 + 1 = two Buddhas become one Buddha in the 0 and live
an eternally happy life!

100. September 20, 1992. Paris

1. Never say things which others do not want to hear.
2. Never say things which make others unhappy.
3. Do not be boastful.
4. Speaking honestly is good, but if what you say disturbs and creates delusion for others, that is not correct.
5. Do not say things to make others jealous.
6. Between lovers, do not speak about your past lovers and do not compare them to your present lover.
7. All the above ways of speech make large blockages in relationships.

Practice people: always be clear so that no kind of speech hinders you. Keep yourself quiescent and always try to help people who speak in the above ways. Show them correct speech and action so that they may realize themselves.

Lovers especially should not waste their time and energy on incorrect speech. Most importantly, do not speak to your lover about the feelings which you had or have for other men or women. Whenever you are together, only speak about how to make a happy, bright and correct life together now and in the future, and about your love and respect for one another. Only talk of beautiful and happy things.

This is the path of having an infinitely happy life and the path which leads to truth.

101. September 20, 1992. Paris

The high and clear autumn sky is incalculably high and clear. But why is my mind not like that? What is blocking it, and to what am I attaching that I feel this way?

In this blocked and attached present life, I yearn to have an incalculably high and clear mind. Sometimes my mind is momentarily high and clear, but it then returns to the karmic level. Instead of the feeling of the incalculably high and clear autumn sky, the cold wind suddenly penetrates my clothes. I become so lonely and I look for the face of my dearly missed lover.

But today my dearly missed lover's face also looks lonely.

Hi! I am here! Do you see?

102. September 21, 1992. Paris

Always beautifully adorn yourself.

With beautiful action, make the lotus flower bloom.

With beautiful thinking, place the lotus blossom on the calm pond.

Always become a white lotus flower. But according to the season, time and moment, change into all different colors—red, blue, yellow—thereby making others' minds happy.

But when night falls, again become a white lotus flower and rest peacefully and comfortably within the closed petals.

Into your most comfortable sanctuary, the o, place and bury all difficulties. In the o, forget and put everything down. Go into the o and relax comfortably with your true lover and share the pillow together.

103. September 22, 1992. Paris

Always keep your mind clear and bright, and do not be hindered anywhere. Keep your vows and go steadfastly forward.

The path of keeping your vows is the way to make yourself happy and complete. Not keeping your vows is the way to self-destruction. The path of keeping your vows is the way to make yourself shine and to become a complete human being.

In your vows you will find happiness.

Completing your vows is the way to find your diamond.

The day you find your diamond is the day you will become Buddha.

The day the diamond shines is the day you will be able to save all sentient beings.

The day you can give your diamond to your lover is the day you will become infinitely happy.

This is human beings' true happiness. So everyday repeat and recite your vows.

104. September 22, 1992. Paris

In the mind which is like a calm and tranquil river, what shall I create today? Shall I throw small stones and listen to the "plop" sounds? Or shall I throw large rocks and listen to the "SHHPLOSH!" sounds? No! I will put beautiful, small and cute onyx stones in there one by one. With them, I will build in my beautiful mind a stupa to Buddha.

What shall I put in Buddha's stupa? Ahh! I will put my vows in there, and I will do my mantra every day so that my vows will become true.

Na Mu Kwan Se Um Bo Sal
Na Mu So Ga Mo Ni Bul
Chong Gak Mio Poep Yon Hwa Kyong

Wow! Why is it that the mantra is so clear today?

105. September 22, 1992. Paris

I always fly freely from this planet to that planet, and from that planet to this planet.

But when I approached this particular planet, it was obscured by clouds. I wondered why I could not see clearly. Those clouds were the pollution of 5 billion human beings' 84,000 delusions, making a total of 420,000,000,000,000 (420 trillion) clouds covering the planet. That is why this planet was difficult to approach.

I was going to give up, but because I was curious I penetrated through the clouds and came here. My body was very sticky and I felt as though I was stepping in mud.

While I was walking through the mud, my shoes came off here and there. They came off in many different places and now they are everywhere.

So every week, I return to find my shoes. I put them back on, remove the mud, and make a beautiful Buddha land.

When I put my shoes back on, dust comes off them. That makes me uncomfortable. But while I patiently polish the shoes, they become shinier and much more comfortable than they were before.

Today I am going to go find the shoes that I left behind on Ahabah Mountain and see if they have become dusty or if they are as shiny as they were when I last left. I will see!

106. September 23, 1992. Barcelona

In the clear, bright and shining place, happiness is overflowing like a waterfall. How can I express this happiness? It cannot be done through words or speech.

In the happy place, become one with your lover and always sit comfortably in this mind and body.

Wherever I go, whatever I do, whoever I meet, I always feel immeasurably secure. When I want to see my lover, I see the lover who is inside of my mind; when I wish to speak, I speak with my lover who is inside of my mind. There are no hindrances or blockages, and what flows are only smiles and happiness. I truly appreciate the love of, and being together with, my lover.

All the sufferings and difficulties I have experienced until now arose and were endured in order to be able to come together with and more greatly appreciate my lover. Also, all the practice that I have done until now was done so that I could be united with my lover.

I am inside of my lover and my lover is inside of me. Two become one and shine throughout the entire world. All darkness disappears from the valleys, mountains and meadows. Everyone is so happy and greets us with love and appreciation. In all places, love and happiness bloom like a flower, and the fragrance of the whole world is so sweet and full.

Mmmmmm!! It smells so good!
(*'Lover' is Buddha, truth, absolute.*)

107. September 23, 1992. Barcelona

Parting the clouds, I fly in the sky and forget all delusions. I put everything down and my mind and body fly. In this moment, I become one with Buddha.

In the o, time and space are immeasurable. With Buddha's wide and immeasurable supernatural power, all the sentient beings covered by clouds are helped. I invite everyone to come into infinite time and space to have the taste and experience of this moment.

I do not know why sentient beings who have many conditions and a lot of karma hesitate so much. Their hesitation perturbs me. HELLO!!

Please put everything down and look here! Can you see this face smiling at you or can you not? Bury all in the mantra, enter the bright, clear and beautiful place, and have an infinitely joyous and wonderful life.

$$1 + 1 = \left(\begin{array}{c}\text{infinite time}\\\text{infinite space}\end{array}\right)$$

108. September 24, 1992. Ahabah

Why does the lotus flower purposely bloom in the dirty, dirty pond? It sinks its roots into the dirt and from there grows up to rise above the water. To do so, it must go through much difficulty and suffering.

But it endures, overcoming all difficulties. And as it rises above the water, blooming beautifully, it makes others' minds happy and beauteous.

Human beings are the same. When they must live in this difficult world and eliminate their karma, it is not easy. But if they endure, practicing through their difficulties, they will ultimately find their true selves. Having found their truth, they always make others happy and joyous. This is human beings' correct path; it is just like that of a lotus flower.

The Buddha said: attain enlightenment and help others. While you wait to meet your lover whom you yearn for so much, clean your mind and body. Having cleaned yourself, when you meet your lover you will make each other happy. When one couple is happy, ten thousand people are happy.

109. September 24, 1992. Ahabah

The mind which has faith in others is the mind which has faith in oneself.
The mind which is for others is the mind which is for oneself.
The mind which does not have faith in others is the mind which does not have faith in oneself.
The mind which is not for others is the mind which is not for oneself.
The mind which hates others is the mind which hates oneself.
The mind which loves others is the mind which loves oneself.
The mind which makes others happy is the mind which makes oneself happy.

Remember all of this and break through your wall of karma. Make an embroidery of beauty and love in your mind. Live life beautifully, without loneliness.

110. September 25, 1992. Ahabah

When someone has confidence in you and entrusts you with all, do not become arrogant or feel self-important because you received that position and trust. You must respect and be thankful to the person who gave you that opportunity and recognize his wide, glorious mind. To make happy the person who trusts and gives you a position, strive to do your best for him.

It is the same for all relationships. When the wife trusts her husband and the husband trusts his wife and they give everything to one another, they must not become arrogant. The wife should be thankful to her husband who trusts her, and the husband should be thankful to his wife who trusts him. They must respect the mutual trust they have in one another and strive to do their best in the obligations which they have for each other. This is the path which leads to infinitely happy relationships.

111. September 25, 1992. Ahabah

When I trust you, I am trusting ten thousand people outside.
When I make you happy, I am making happy ten thousand people outside.
When I care for you, I am caring for ten thousand people outside.

> When I fully understand you, I am fully understanding ten thousand people outside.
> When I embrace you, I am embracing ten thousand people outside.
> When I truly love you, I am truly loving ten thousand people outside.
> When I make you as a Buddha, I am making as Buddhas ten thousand people outside.
> When I become your wife, I am becoming the wife of ten thousand people outside.
> When you become my husband, you are becoming the husband of ten thousand people outside.

In the clear and bright place, the theory of nature is that the union of yin (–) and yang (+) energies creates this world. So when I become one with you, we build and adorn with true beauty a true world and Buddha land.

Precious you, please be eternally comfortable, tranquil and happy.

112. September 26, 1992. Ahabah

Always be satisfied with yourself, every day. Whoever knows how to be satisfied with himself or herself is someone who knows the path of happiness and who will be successful. But whoever is not satisfied with himself or herself will lose even the small happiness that he or she has and fall into the path of suffering.

> Be satisfied with the people you know and are presently with.
> Be satisfied with your master or teacher.

Be satisfied with your husband or wife.

Be satisfied with your friends and relatives.

If you know how to be satisfied with others, you will always be respected by many people and will know how to make your present life a paradise and how to enjoy it. But if you always complain about and discriminate against others, you will never know what paradise is. You will always go to the path of suffering and will not know how to get out.

Practice people: learn how to give love to others and how to respect others in this present life. This is the path of Buddha.

113. September 26, 1992. Ahabah

We always live in absolute love.

We always live in absolute happiness.

But we were sinking into thick karma and therefore did not know what true happiness is; we had the habit of living in our thick karma. For that reason, even if you came out from your karma and into a truly joyous situation, you missed being in your karma and tried to transplant your unhappy situation into your happy one. Because you were unable to know whether you were happy or not, you had difficulty realizing and experiencing your present happiness and you tried to go back to your thick karma world.

Enjoy your present happiness now as much as you can. Go one more step into happiness and have a truly happy life, without fears or hindrances.

114. September 27, 1992. Ahabah

In the Lotus Sutra it says, "One is in the many, many are in the one." When one person gives his or her mind and body to one person, that vow is the most glorious and wonderful thing.

Our body is made from karma. Therefore, our mind is tainted by karma, and we are far away from our true place. Being always in the karma place, we live life equivocally. We live insecurely and have many kinds of suffering.

The person who gives his or her entire life to the person he or she loves, with trust and respect, that is someone who can find the true, original place. To have another to give your life and everything to, that is to be the happiest person in the world.

When the student dedicates his or her life to the master, when the wife dedicates her life to her husband, when the husband dedicates his life to his wife, and when lovers also do so, this giving of everything to another is the most beautiful thing in the world.

Two becoming one is the path of Buddha. Engaging many other people as that one which came from two is the path of saving sentient beings.

115. September 27, 1992. Ahabah

I practice for you.
I work for you.
I study for you.
I sleep for you.
I wash my body for you.
I eat for you.

I make my mind beautiful for you.
Whenever, wherever and whatever I do, it is all for you. I live for you.

The satisfaction, completion, happiness and contentment which come from the union of yin and yang is reaching Buddha's absolute, original place. When I become one with you, that is the place of Buddha. This place has no conditions or desires, and it is where two people may truly love one another. This is the place where you can enjoy happiness 24 hours or 1,440 minutes per day.

116. September 28, 1992. Paris

Great Vow

117. September 29, 1992. Paris

In the rice patch, the plants that receive lots of love become ripe, and the heads of these plants all bow down. But the plants in the rice patch that do not receive enough love always stand straight and stiff.

It is the same with people. Those who do not receive a lot of love are always arrogant, have a lot of desire and like to show off.

But those who receive true love from others become very humble, lower themselves for others, and fulfill their responsibilities meticulously and beautifully. When others see such people, they truly respect them.

Those who have not yet received true love from others should please practice vigorously, polish themselves, and have true concern and care for others.

Whoever has received true love should always be thankful for it, practice regularly and make that love shine more brightly.

118. September 29, 1992. Paris

A Buddha is a sentient being who does not speak.

A sentient being is a Buddha who speaks.

When you do not speak, you become a Buddha; when you do not think, you become a Buddha; when you do not act, you become a Buddha.

When a sentient being speaks, always speak like a Buddha.

When a sentient being thinks, always think like a Buddha.

When a sentient being acts, always act like a Buddha.

But when you speak, do so for the benefit of others and in order to make them happy; when you think, eliminate all of your desire, delusion and ego; realizing non-self, only think about how to make others happy; and when you act, only act to help others.

119. September 30, 1992. Paris

Even though you are clear and bright, when you are in the situation of falling in love it is difficult to retain your clarity and brightness.

Because you want to please your loved one and make that person as happy as possible, your attachment makes the bright and clear place dull. At times, the attachment of wanting to please your loved one may even turn your mind sychophantic. That mind can make your loved one very uncomfortable and can cause you to become discontented with yourself because the bright and clear place has lost its luster.

Take the attached and sycophantic minds which come from love and place them one step further into the bright and clear place. There, live an unexcelled, happy life, sharing true, absolute, infinite love together.

120. September 30, 1992. Paris

Human relations are such that when you only think about your own position and pride, it is difficult to have good relations with others.

Always engage your situation according to the circumstances and act according to the people you are with. But at the same time do not forget to retain the bright and clear place.

When you deal with children, become a child for them; when you deal with adults, become an adult for them; when you deal with your husband or wife, become a husband or wife for that person.

Wherever you are and whoever you are with, do not be proud and do not impose yourself and your position on others. Always live flexibly, according with each situation, transforming and displaying yourself in accordance with others' needs, levels and dispositions. Also, do not be hindered by your age. Live an ageless and completely free life.

Here is a little story. One evening, Queen Victoria of Great Britain wanted to visit her husband, Prince Albert, in his private chamber. She knocked on his door and he asked, "Who is it?" She replied, "The Queen of Great Britain." To this he said, "I'm sorry, but I do not know that woman," and refused to open the door. The Queen went away in a huff.

She tried again the following evening. She knocked on the door and Prince Albert asked, "Hello. Who is it?" This time she answered, "Queen Victoria." Through the closed door he said, "I'm sorry, but I do not know her." Once again she went away, angrier and more humiliated than the evening before.

The next night she again knocked on her husband's door. He asked, "Who is it?" The Queen replied, "Your wife!" Prince Albert opened the door and said, "Oh!! Please come in."

121. October 1, 1992. Rhein Ruhr

Always give rise to the mind which understands others.
    This is the path of protecting oneself.
Always know how to compliment others. This is the path
    of being respected by others.
When you do not have an understanding mind for others,
    this leads to your being lonely.
When you complain about others, this leads to your losing
    credit and being deceived by others.
When you check others, this will lead to your not receiving love from others.

Life seems to be difficult, but bury everything in the bright and clear place, and try to find the truth within quiescence. Then life becomes easier and each thing you do, one by one, becomes very interesting.

And do not forget, one always exists by and through others.

122. October 1, 1992. Rhein Ruhr

Do not doubt others. Doubt gives rise to anxiety and that comes back to the person who doubts others.

Also, do not dig into the doubts of people who made doubtful actions. Take one step back from their actions and forgive and have pity for them.

It is due to having a lot of karma that people act doubtfully to others. Practice for such people so that they do not act doubtfully again. Care greatly for them so that they will become beautiful human beings.

Remember, the tree which fully receives love rain always stands straight, is clear and grows beautifully. But the tree which does not fully receive love rain always grows crookedly, shrivels and is not beautiful.

123. October 2, 1992. Rhein Ruhr

Married people: do not commit adultery. And unmarried people: do not change your girlfriend or boyfriend so much. Sexual desire comes from bodily desire and not from the truth.

Becoming a couple means having a special connection with your partner. So even though you may at times have difficulties with your partner, you must overcome them and make a true relationship and have true love together. Become a happy, absolute and true couple; this is true happiness.

When you look at passages on karma in the sutras, you will find it said that people who make love with many different partners will be reborn as dogs in their next lives. I know that this is absolutely true.

So eliminate your sexual desire and purify yourself. This is very important, because if you have sexual desire you cannot meet your true partner and you cannot have true love.

Always seek true love which is beyond sexual desire. When you attain the truth, you will meet your true partner, and then you can have true sex together.

True sex comes from a pure and clear place, and is true love conversation. It is a sharing of great love energy through which a couple supports and protects one another. This sharing gives great satisfaction and appreciation of one's present form, which comes from a true place.

If you would like to have this, do not commit adultery or change your girlfriend or boyfriend too much. If you do these things, you will become dirty and you will suffer eternally. So eliminate your sexual desire, become clear and bright, and create a complete, true love relationship with your partner.

124. October 3, 1992. Rhein Ruhr
The path is everywhere.
What is the true path?

A long time ago someone asked a master, "What is the path?" The master answered, "Clouds are in the sky, water is in the water bottle."

What does this mean?

The path is everywhere.

Do not forget to keep your position. For example, the master keeps the master's position, the student keeps the student's position, the husband keeps the husband's position, the wife keeps the wife's position. Always keep your position and do your sincere, best job.

That path is very smooth and is the path of Buddha.

But there are circumstances in which a teacher can be a student, a student can be a master, a husband can be a wife and a wife can be a husband. What does this mean? And, what is the meaning of "the path is 'clouds are in the sky, water is in the water bottle'"?

125. October 3, 1992. Rhein Ruhr

Masters always practice for their students.
Students always practice for their master.
A wife always practices for her husband.
A husband always practices for his wife.
Parents always practice for their children.
Children always practice for their parents.
Friends always practice for their friends.
Lovers always practice for their lover.

Practice mind is Buddha and bodhisattva mind. When you do things for others, you become clear and bright and your karma is automatically eliminated. When you live for others with this bright mind, this present world becomes beautiful and happiness springs up like a fountain.

126. October 4, 1992. Rhein Ruhr

Whoever wants many things must practice.
Whoever does not want anything must practice.
Whoever wants many things: practice until you get what you want.
Whoever does not want anything: practice until something appears which you do want.

Even though you get what you want, continue practicing in order to be able to appreciate and keep eternally that which you received.

Practice is to find oneself.
Practice is to eliminate that which you found.
Practice until you completely annihilate what you are.
Practice within that annihilated self until you make others happy.
Practice to see that those whom you made happy are truly happy and that they are on the path of Buddha.
Practice for those who are on the path of Buddha until they become a Buddha.

Then you may take a vacation.

127. October 5, 1992. Paris

The bright and clear mind is Buddha-mind; that mind makes you become a Buddha.

Unclear mind, egotistical mind, playing-games mind and calculating-high-and-low mind are the minds of sentient beings; they make you become a sentient being.

Always bury yourself in the 0. Without hoping for something in return, always do your best in your everyday work. Then everything you want will automatically appear, you will become Buddha, and you will always live a beautiful life.

1 means 'I'; that is, karma I.

1 + 1 is the conditional world; that is, the suffering world.

1 + 0 is the unconditional world; that is, the very comfortable world.

Do not make '1 + 1'.

Next to '1' always put 0 and make 0. Think and live in the 0. This is the inside of Buddha and is true I.

128. October 6, Paris

There is an I that lives in the midst of love, that lives in the midst of truth, and that lives in the midst of brightness and clarity.

In there, if I want to be the most beautiful woman in the world, I become the most beautiful woman in the world. In there, if I want to be a wife, I can be the most wonderful wife in the world. In there, if I want to be a great master, I can be the greatest master in the world. In there, if I want to be a mother, I can be the most caring mother in the world. In there, I can be a friend, a lover, and so on.

In there, you can be anything that you want to be. This is living inside of the diamond.

A long time ago, a dragon practiced for hundreds of years to get this diamond. When he got it, he became completely free and ascended to the sky.

The inside of the diamond is what we call diamond energy. This energy can do anything.

Dear practitioner: please practice and find the diamond as soon as possible and realize how to use it. The reason why I am teaching you every day is to help you to get this diamond.

129. October 7, 1992. Paris

People who are in love and people who want to be loved: always keep your mind bright and clear. When one person suffers, the other also suffers; when one person is happy, the other is also happy.

Always stay happy together with loving, caring and helping mind. Keep your mind bright and clear, and together become a clear, cloudless sky, living every day happily, forever.

130. October 7, 1992. Paris

Love Letter

Your broad mind which endures all difficulties only wants to make me happy; your trusting mind entrusts me with everything; your concerned mind tries to not let me suffer even a tiny bit; and your mind of endurance tries to make everything smooth.

I sincerely thank you for your profound, great love.

Your beautiful, glorious and wonderful mind touches me and makes me so happy. This happy mind makes me into a great bodhisattva.

Today and forevermore, I bring forth happy smiles on my face, automatically helping others, and thus this world becomes a Buddha-land adorned with beauty.

I always love you infinitely and I sincerely appreciate your true, great love.

131. October 8, 1992. Paris

Whoever wants to find the correct path of life, whoever wants happiness and whoever wants to receive admiration from others: always look into yourself.

See what your thinking is now: is it bad or is it good? Also, be aware of what you are saying. Is your speech helping others or is it making a show of yourself? Is it disdainful or sycophantic? Look at your present actions. Are you keeping your correct position as a husband, wife, lover, student and so on?

Touching and hugging a man or woman who is not your partner makes both of you confused and creates inappropriate desire. Through this you waste a lot of energy, suffering appears and your path becomes unclear. To prevent this in ancient times, men and women who were strangers to one another did not even make eye contact.

Practice people: when you meet anyone other than your correct partner, do not greet him or her with a hug or a kiss. Always put your hands together and greet them with a *hapchang*. This is the way to keep clear, to receive much admiration from others, to not make unnecessary karma and to keep your energy correctly.

Follow this path and realize why you do mirror practice every morning.

132. October 9, 1992. Frankfurt

Following the path of practice and following the path which leads to becoming a Buddha is not difficult. But to eliminate your karma, throwing away your opinions and following the teachings, is difficult.

The path of practice is very near and the day of becoming a Buddha is not far off for those who are able to follow the teachings. But those who have a lot of discrimination, opinions and judgments about the teachings must practice harder. They must perceive the mind that makes right and wrong, and find the mind that is before discrimination.

If wise people have some doubt about a teaching, they acquiesce to and practice that teaching, making it their own, and then teach others through the experience they have had. Then they truly appreciate the importance of the teaching they had previously doubted, and it brightly shines. With greatly dawning admiration for their master, they also appreciate their own wisdom that enabled them to discover what they had not known before.

Remember: the bitterer the medicine is, the better it is for the body. The master becomes smarter through difficult and doubting students, and these students become smarter through the strength and strictness of their master.

Wise students always appreciate their strong and strict master's great wisdom and fearless courage; they *hapchang* and bow their heads in great appreciation for their master.

P.S. My master was the hardest and strictest teacher. But one day I discovered that behind his strictness was great love and compassion. The moment I discovered that, I realized and attained what true love is.

133. October 10, 1992. Frankfurt

An unwise person always makes unwise relationships and suffers from this.

For example, one man who has a lot of attachment and desire only sees the exterior beauty of a particular woman's form and indulges in desiring her. Because he is so attracted to this woman, he wishes her to like him, but she is also unwise and only sees the man's exterior form. Because he is not as handsome as she would like, she does not desire him. Of course, she knows that he likes her, but she only wants to use him, playing games with him, disparaging him and treating him very badly. Because of her treatment, he loses other people's respect, and so through his own desires loses his position. Because others do not respect him, he feels terrible about himself.

Whoever is in this kind of situation, please eliminate your attachments and desires as soon as possible and follow the true path.

A man who has a lot of desire does not know which women are truly beautiful. Always be clear and bright and find a partner who truly appreciates you and to whom you can give true love. Make a true relationship and have true love together, without desire. Then you will be well respected by others.

Whoever does not eliminate their desires suffers eternally, makes very bad karma, and hurts both themselves and others.

If you can truly love your partner, you can discover true beauty behind exterior form. Discovering that, your relationship will last eternally. With that beautiful love you will make all others happy. *(This teaching applies equally to women as it does to men.)*

134. October 11, 1992. Frankfurt

The tongue has no bone. But an ignorant mind always puts a bone inside of the tongue. That bone pokes others' hearts terribly and in return also hurts very badly the person who made it.

Always be careful of your speech. That is very important. Especially in close relationships, be careful of how you express yourself so that you do not make one another suffer. If you express yourself using bad speech, those words go into the other person's consciousness, causing suffering for them as well as for you.

There is always a 'devil' inside of an ignorant and unclear mind. That 'devil' causes suffering for you and for others. Before you speak, first eliminate your 'devil' and lack of clarity. Secondly, be careful of what you say.

Especially lovers, be careful of your speech; bad speech can demolish true love and a true relationship. Speaking honestly is good, but before you open your mouth, check and see if you have a 'devil' inside of yourself.

Meeting your true partner and having true love together is due to the good karma that you made by practicing for many lives. The love and relationship for which you worked so long and hard can be destroyed by just one sentence of wrong speech, and that single utterance can cause you to live the rest of your life in great loneliness.

Those who have a lot of devil mind inside of them do not know what true beauty and true feelings of love are. It is as though their eyes are obscured by thick glasses.

So, if you are not clear, remove the bone from your tongue.

135. October 12, 1992. Paris
[This is Dae Poep Sa Nim's teaching for today.]

136. October 13, 1992. Paris
When you look at the karmic record, a person who causes terrible pain to another's heart becomes a slave, if not in this life then in the next life, to the person whom he hurt.

Those who hurt others usually have a lot of desires and ego, and that is why they always criticize others. For example, there is a man who never received true love before. But he practiced last life and does so presently, too. With the virtue he made through practicing, he meets, for the first time, his true partner from whom he receives true love. But because his bad karma still follows him, he has difficulty accepting and digesting that true love. He believes that he is extraordinarily good and high and assumes that is why he has received this love. Instead of appreciation, his pride and arrogance grow; and instead of respecting the one who loves him, he plays games with her and causes her pain. Because his ego has become bigger, he tries to find something better than the true love and thus creates more bad karma for himself.

This situation is just like a very thirsty man in the hot desert. When he comes upon an oasis, he is so grateful and happy to drink the water. But after he has quenched his thirst, rather than appreciating the oasis, he complains that the water did not taste good.

Remember: practice vigorously and do not become like this kind of person. Always be bright and clear and live a truly beautiful life.

137. October 13, 1992. Paris

Put the o bandage on the deeply scarred heart.

But the scar aches and stings, and I don't want to put the o bandage on it. I fight with myself, resisting. But one day, someone with a loving hand comes and without saying a word puts the o bandage over the scar. At first, I am angry, but afterwards the scar and pain disappear without my knowing it, and the place where the scar was is soothed and restored.

Just then, Buddha is before me, gazing at me and smiling. "How are you?" he asks. Without even thinking about it, I reply, "I'm fine."

138. October 14, 1992. Paris

Having faith is the fastest way to eliminate one's karma. Faithful mind is Buddha's mind.

Build up your faith. Whoever has faith is on the Buddha path, eliminating their 84,000 delusions and desires. The time of becoming a Buddha is not far off for them.

Bury everything—your ego, delusions and desires—inside of the faithful mind and go into 0 as soon as possible. Then, without faith, have a faithful relationship and without thinking about faith, have a truly faithful life.

139. October 14, 1992. Paris

Searching in the dark night…. But just because it is dark, do not suffer and do not give up your search.

When you are in darkness, completely engross your mind in trying to find Buddha. Keep that mind and practice. In that moment of complete engrossment, darkness disappears and suddenly the bright sun appears. Right there, darkness cleanly vanishes. Completely relax in the bright sun's warmth and forget about all of your past sufferings.

Practice and go into Buddha's place. Realize that you make darkness and brightness. Become master of yourself and do not be hindered by darkness or brightness. Live your life without suffering.

When you are in darkness, perceive yourself more clearly. When you are in brightness, perceive why you have that good situation and make your life the way you want it to be.

140. October 15, 1992. Paris

Everything is created by the mind alone. Thirteen hundred years ago in Korea, there lived a great master named Won Hyo. One night, while on a journey in China he was very thirsty and searched for water in the dark. All of a sudden, he found a bowl with water inside of it, which he drank and greatly appreciated. That night he slept very peacefully. When he awoke the next morning after sunrise, he saw that the water bowl was actually a dirty, broken human skull. When he saw what he had drunk from, he attained enlightenment and realized that everything is created by the mind alone.

No matter how difficult your situation is, if you keep a positive mind, a positive life appears. However, if your thinking is ugly, even though you meet a beautiful person, that person is ugly to you. But if your thinking is beautiful, even an ugly person is beautiful. This is the theory of the mind.

First, perceive the mind which is seeing. Second, perceive the mind which sees that mind.

The mind which sees through karma and the mind which sees through the truth are different. When the mind is in the clear and bright 0, it is not hindered by any karma, devils or discrimination, and it can see true beauty.

In the eyes of a person who has a lot of karma, a genuine diamond looks fake. Such people lose the true diamond and suffer for the rest of their lives. But in the bright mind of the bright person who has attained 0, even if a fake diamond should appear, his or her brightness and clarity will turn it into a true diamond. A bright and clear person can always create a beautiful life, living as he or she wishes.

141. October 16, 1992. Paris

In the bright and clear place:
1. Perceive the form which creates difficulties.
2. Perceive the thinking which makes that form function.
3. Perceive the mind which creates that thinking.
4. Perceive the mind which gives rise to that mind.
5. Perceive the mind which, even though you look, is no-mind.
6. When you realize that there is no-mind, perceive what makes this form suffer and what makes it happy.
7. Perceive what you are doing now.
8. Perceive your thinking in this moment. Is it bothering others, is it jealous of others, or is it loving of others?
9. Forget everything and think that you are happy.
10. What are your responsibilities in this moment? See what you must do right now and do it.

142. October 17, 1992. Paris

People who can perceive themselves are the ones who are ready for the path of Buddha.

People who perceive themselves for even just one day are the ones who are already on the path of Buddha.

People who can perceive themselves are the ones who can eliminate their karma.

People who perceive themselves are the ones who already watch what appears daily in their minds.

When you can perceive everything, it is so interesting that it is inexpressible.

Perceive yourself, remove your bad characteristics, keep the good ones, and share the good with others. Go deeply into your self-perception, make yourself as clear as a mirror, and make use of yourself in an appreciative way, moment to moment. This is the true way to live life.

143. October 18, 1992. Paris

When you know one person, you know 10,000 people. When you do not know one person, you do not know yourself or others.

Going into the o is the work of each individual; by going into the o one eliminates one's karma, delusions, ego and attachments, and finds one's true self and true I.

First, find who you are.

When you know the o you will know one person. When you are able to meet one person, it is because he is already in the o.

People who do not know the o do not know themselves or others.

When you know the o and you meet one person whom you can love, care for, and dedicate your life to, you are loving, caring and living for 10,000 people.

When you give your entire life to one person, you know what true love and happiness are. Then you can also appreciate and be proud of yourself and really know the true taste of life.

144. October 19, 1992. Paris

To get money, food, fame, sex and sleep is very easy. But to meet one true person is very difficult. Meeting one true person is your reward for the practice you have done in previous lives as well as for what you have done in this life.

When you meet that one true person, your needs for money, food, fame, sex and sleep will be satisfied.

So please practice regularly and vigorously and meet your true person. Then you can live this life as you want and be eternally happy.

(Note: your true person can, for example, be a master, a student, a wife, a husband or a lover.)

145. October 20, 1992. Paris

The Buddha said, "Do not trust human beings; do not trust even me. Only trust and rely upon the Dharma."

The Dharma is the truth and true I and is the o. Always be mindful of, have trust and faith in, and live your life depending upon the o.

But who is transmitting the Dharma? The Buddha and the masters are. Depend upon the masters' Dharma teaching and be supported by their energy, which is also Dharma. It is for these teachings and energy that we respect the Buddha and the masters. Trusting their teaching, we find our true selves.

When you bow to me, Ji Kwang Dae Poep Sa Nim, it is not I who receive your prostration; it is the Dharma that receives your prostration. That is because the Dharma is spread and energy is transmitted through this form body.

146. October 21, 1992. Paris

In the quiescent place, live life quiescently, and leave (die) quiescently. This is the path of Buddha.

In the complicated place, live a complicated life, and leave (die) in a complicated way. This is the path of sentient beings.

Even if you are in a complicated world, keep your mind quiescent; and if you have a complicated life, live quiescently. Then, even if you must leave (die) in a complicated way, you can go freely. This is the path of practice.

If the person who practices dwells in a quiescent place but does not know what the path of practice truly is, he or she feels bored rather than appreciative. Such people could live very quiescently and comfortably, but always make their lives very uncomfortable, creating lots of suffering. Even though they could leave (die) quiescently, they leave in a complicated way, bothering others.

The path of practice is without ego, without criticism, and without showing off. The person on this path is always humble and always respects others. This is the way and life of the practice person and is complete quiescence.

147. October 22, 1992. Vienna

The colorful Buddha and the diamond Buddha.
Shinier and brighter than the sun and moon Buddha.

O is not just white. It is the beautiful place, just like the colorful Buddha, the shining Buddha and the diamond Buddha. Dwell within this beautiful o. In there, where do suffering, difficulties, sadness, and blockages exist?

Always think, speak and act within this beautiful o and live your life very colorfully.

When you think, speak and act from within this beautiful place, that is saving others.

148. October 23, 1992. Vienna

The path of wise persons is very clear. They always steadfastly follow the path of the vows they have taken. As they go, they are not hindered by any difficulties or by criticism from others; they just go straight ahead without wavering and keep their vows successfully.

Unwise people know what the clear path is, but are always shaken by criticism from others and hindered by their influence. As a result, such people make the path very unclear, and because they are shaken, they are unsuccessful and drown in their own karma.

Practicing people always make themselves strong so that no outside devils can come inside of them. Remember: a weak roof always leaks rain and shakes in the wind.

Make your mind like a strong and sturdy roof so that no outside devils can infiltrate you. Steadfastly follow your path without speech and without double thinking.

Remember, for example, that your true friend always tries to help you follow your path. Untrue friends may appear helpful on the outside, but on the inside they want to block you from following your path. That is why the Buddha recommended closing your eyes, ears and mouth once you have committed to practice and just following your path.

149. October 24, 1992. Vienna

Always remember and single-mindedly think about the beautiful o place.

Whoever sees the beauty in himself or herself sees the beauty in others. When you see others' beauty, all of your own suffering disappears.

Within the non-suffering o place, fulfill your work as best as you can each day, and live life beautifully.

An ugly person sees others as ugly and makes suffering for them.

Give rise to a beautiful mind, eliminate your karma, and beautifully adorn this present life. This is the path of practice.

150. October 24, 1992. Vienna

Within the happy o, always think about and plan for happiness. Pursue happiness and then everything will become happy.

Within the happy o place, why must one think about unhappy things, getting caught up in and frightened by unhappiness?

Bury all of your delusions and bad experiences and memories of the past into the happy o place. From this moment on, only think about happiness and put it into happy action. Then everything will become happy, contented and satisfied.

151. October 25, 1992. Vienna

The dharma center is the place of truth and energy. Living there means seeking the truth, finding your true I, and practicing to become free from karma and to become a completely free person. Not everyone may have this opportunity; it only comes for those who have special karma. Do not waste this opportunity, and appreciate that you have the chance to live there.

Remember: the dharma center is where true love and compassion are. Practice vigorously there and make yourself become successful.

Someone who lives in a dharma center but does not practice, who becomes lazy and idle, and does not abide by the rules is a bother to others. No matter where this kind of person goes in the outside world he or she will not be welcomed by others and will create a suffering life.

If you live in a dharma center, try to eliminate your daily difficulties. Use this great opportunity to attain truth and Buddhahood, and to live your life freely and clearly.

152. October 26, 1992. Paris

To become a Buddha and help all sentient beings, monks vow to transcend yin and yang, including relationships between men and women. A monk practices vigorously in order to be together with Buddha, always.

Once a monk becomes a Buddha, for the purpose of saving sentient beings, he returns to their level, directly teaching and guiding them by adopting appropriate appearances and positions according to their needs.

If after becoming a Buddha, one wishes to teach only monks, one remains a monk and teaches them. This might be called Mahayana Buddhism.

Once you know the o place, teaching about that might be called Zen Buddhism.

In Social Buddhism, after you become a Buddha, if you wish to teach wives, you become a wife; if you wish to teach husbands, you become a husband; if you wish to teach parents, you become a parent, etc. Having attained non-self through practice, you exist in this world only to teach, help and show others how to live correctly. Therefore, in our sangha we use many different means to save people at different levels from their suffering.

153. October 27, 1992. Paris

To earn and attain the o place, throw away your body, mind, desires, ego, delusions and everything. Having attained this place, what is my duty right now?

In order to attain and earn this place I revolved many times between the earth and the sky, creating and experiencing many sufferings, imaginary things, fantasies and projections. Finally I earned and attained the o.

In this o place, what shall I do and for whom shall I live? I live for my lovely students, I live for my lovely husband, I live for my lovely children, I live for my lovely friends and everybody. This life is truly appreciative and is without taint. This life is the bodhisattva life and is the great, universal and free life.

154. October 28, 1992. Paris

Human beings' thinking is various. But they always think that what they know is the best. So, when things do not go the way they expected, they become angry, they bother others, and they suffer. They resort to their own karma, not knowing what is right and wrong, and go back to suffering and living very difficult lives.

Before practice persons express their ideas they always put their thinking into the o, see if their thinking is right or wrong, and then put it into action.

When there is no right and wrong, and nothing to think about: go into action through the o without speaking.

And remember, when you go one step forward, always go one step back and only then express your idea and thinking. This action is to help others, to protect yourself and to have a secure life.

155. October 29, 1992. On the train to Geneva

True bodhisattva action and mind are unconditional action and unconditional mind. Throw away your self, throw away your conditions and only act for others.

Doing this is just like what happens when you try to please a crying baby: your body and mind are entirely involved in giving the baby what he or she wants. Because you have the mind to make the baby as comfortable as possible, you forget about your own tiredness, you forget about your pain, you forget about all of your own conditions and are totally absorbed in stopping the baby's crying.

When the baby is finally sleeping comfortably, you relax. Gazing at the face of the sleeping baby, your mind feels very comfortable and happy.

Whoever can use this bodhisattva mind and action at home, in his social life, and in his group life is already on the path of Buddha and is on his way to becoming a Buddha himself.

Throw away your own conditions; unconditionally want only to make others happy. This kind of action is true human beings' action; and this kind of mind is the mind human beings are supposed to have. Whoever has this kind of mind and action has already eliminated his own karma and is free and liberated.

I will use this form, which is going to decay and rot, very appreciatively for others.

I will use this mind, which is going to disappear, to make others happy, and I will use it beautifully every day.

156. October 30, 1992. Geneva

The spoon does not know the taste of the soup. Just so, although truth is ever-present, people often do not know the truth even if they act as if they do. In fact, they do not know how to act, think, or speak truthfully. They may want to go for the truth, but they always fall into the devil world and act, think, and speak like a devil. This sends them into suffering, causes suffering for others, and creates such an unhappy life.

Truth does not have I, my, me. Truth is the mind which can entrust everything to others and which can give everything to others without conditions. This is the way of going into the true world and of finding big I, which is true I. True life is when, without karma, you only make others happy and their happiness is your happiness.

Whoever wants the truth must first eliminate his or her ego. An egotistical person does not know the taste of the truth and cannot truly enter into it.

157. October 31, 1992. Geneva

Whoever has a lot of desires has a lot of faults. Acting out their faults, such people only create more unnecessary desires; they are like hungry people looking for food who only become hungrier in the process.

Wise people have less desire and only want to go in the correct direction. They are like people who are already full; no matter what kind of food you offer, they do not want to eat.

If you have a lot of desires, do not pursue your desires. Before you follow your desires, always see yourself and try to fix your weaknesses. This is the way by which you can eliminate your desires and go in the correct direction of life.

Here is a story: a long time ago there was a person who had many desires and who was very stingy. He always wanted to make lots of money and was saving money. When he had saved $90,000, he decided to try reaching $100,000 and developed a lot of desires about reaching that amount. But every time he got close, he had accidents and crises and could never reach $100,000. Eventually, he lost his original $90,000 and became a beggar.

Another ignorant person who had a beautiful and wise wife had a lot of desires for other women. He lost his beautiful and wise wife, became lonely, and had an infinitely lonely life.

Desire is poison for sentient beings' lives and brings tragedy and infinite suffering. Whenever you have desire mind, perceive that mind right away and work to eliminate it through your practice so that you do not have a suffering and lonely life.

158. November 1, 1992. Geneva

In the beautiful o, I drew my lover's face.

My lover's face was covered by a dark cloud, and my heart trembled.

Though covered by a dark cloud, my lover even then was telling me, "I love you."

Those words made my trembling heart happy.

I always asked Buddha to make my lover's dark cloud disappear.

Buddha accepted my wish and with his supernatural power eliminated my lover's dark cloud.

My lover suddenly became bright and clear, and right away could see me very clearly.

He was so happy to see who I am.

He finally realized who I am.

He rejoiced to discover that I was the person he had been looking for all his life.

He apologized to me, repenting for having sinned by having all kinds of desires and delusions.

He told me, "I love you truly and I will not leave your sight for even one second. I'll be with you forever and ever."

When I looked at my lover's clear and beautiful face, all of the bruises in my heart and all my suffering disappeared.

Without realizing it, I put my lips to his lips, and at that moment all karma disappeared.

Suddenly, this present world became a paradise.

Thank you very much!

159. November 2, 1992. Geneva

Each of the things that comes from the absolute energy place has its own nature. It is like tree leaves: some have a pointed, poky shape while others have a rounded shape. Human beings are also just like this: some people have a poking nature and some have a rounded nature.

But the poky or rounded tree leaves do not disturb others or make them suffer. Each one keeps its own nature and shows nothing but beauty. Human beings behave differently than tree leaves. Instead of creating beauty and shining, people with poky natures always poke others and themselves and creates suffering for all.

Always look into your own nature. Are there any poky things? Are there any rounded things? If you discover a poky thing there, strive to eliminate it. This is the path of practice.

Please live life like a rounded o. That is the absolute, most comfortable life.

160. November 3, 1992. Paris

Twenty-five hundred years ago, Shakyamuni Buddha snapped his fingers and made a very strong sound which spread over the whole world. Through that sound, sentient beings' agony and suffering disappeared.

Twenty-five hundred years later, which is now, when we get up in the morning, instead of making a finger snapping sound we laugh loudly...Ha! Ha! Ha!...and all the agonies, anxieties, delusions, fears, and sufferings disappear.

With a big laugh...Ha! Ha! Ha!...wash away all of your karma. After that moment of washing away your karma, find your o, and in the o, plan your happy day.

161. November 4, 1992. Paris

When bodhisattva mind appears, it means happiness for everybody. But when ego mind appears, it means unhappiness for everybody.

Through doing bodhisattva actions, cut off your desires, delusions, ego and bad karma, and find true o. Make yourself happy with your own happiness and give it to all others; this means happiness for everybody.

Ego always makes one burn; the ego's viper is always poking and hurting others; this means unhappiness for everybody.

The mind of a bodhisattva is that of great love and great compassion. When the bodhisattva mind appears, that means everybody can have this great love and great compassion. This happiness can save the whole world.

Remember that as long as we are sentient beings we all have this bodhisattva mind. So rediscover this bodhisattva mind which is hidden behind our karma and be a bodhisattva 100 percent. This is the path of practice.

162. November 5, 1992. Munich

My body stays in the sentient beings' world. But I rediscover the o and live in the o all of the time, thus living life beyond the human world.

But one day in this *saha* world, I met the person with whom I have a strong connection from my last life, and now I live a 100 percent human life. That taste of life and the experiences I have are very interesting.

Through this experience, I rediscover the inner world of sentient beings' lives much more precisely—their deeper intentions, sufferings and feelings. I realize much more thoroughly what comes from this present form's six senses—its sensations, feelings, and seizures.

I rediscover the mind of anger, the mind of humiliation, the mind of pride. But I also rediscover how, if someone is angry, to change their angry mind into understanding mind, and if someone has a bad feeling, how to change that bad feeling mind into love mind. I also rediscover how to receive and give love correctly, rediscovering the mind of trusting others and the mind of faith.

While having this kind of experience every day, I attain how to give energy to others much more precisely.

I appreciate Bo Haeng Nim who gives me all of this opportunity to have these experiences which make me truly human. With his sincere care, love and comfort, I appreciate him very much.

163. November 6, 1992. Munich

When you make others suffer, you suffer. When you disparage others, you are disparaged yourself. When you try to control others, you become controlled.

When you say that you already know all of these teachings, and so are not interested in them, you become an uninteresting person.

You do not know why you are an uninteresting person. When you say you "don't know," that "don't know" will always cause you and others suffering.

To realize the ignorance of don't-know mind, you must first throw away your ego and build up your mind of respect for others. Do not use don't-know mind as an excuse.

You say, for example, "I know this, but I do not know why it becomes like that." *At that moment, you must realize that you really are an ignorant and stupid person.*

Don't-know ignorance is just like a black cloud that blocks out the sunshine.

Always have the mind that the teaching you are not interested in is actually very important. And always repeat in your mind, just like a mantra: "Ahh! This is very important. This teaching is what I actually need."

164. November 7, 1992. Munich

Because today's world is a computer world people greatly depend on computers and even trust them more than they do themselves. They attach to computers and lose themselves.

Computers and our form bodies are similar. Through the human form's six dusts, six senses and six consciousnesses, we express and emote ourselves; and through energy, we move, just as computers run with electricity.

If we only attach to our form body, that is just like attaching to a computer. So do not attach to what appears from form—sensations, feelings, right and wrong, good and bad. Do not lose yourself by attaching to those things.

Always perceive the mind which moves the form body. Gaze at the mind which moves the form body and which uses the computer, and then use your body and the computer correctly.

Behind the mind, find your true I and that true self which is using this mind. Find that true self and do not be hindered by the mind or by form. Find true liberation and become an absolutely free person.

165. November 8, 1992. Munich

Always go with one.

Practice with one method. Enjoy love with only one person. Have only one master.

A long time ago, countries that had two kings always collapsed, while countries that had only one king always flourished.

When you cannot have devotion to one, you lose yourself and that one too.

When you have devotion to one, you can get everything.

When you continuously practice with one method, you will accomplish Buddhahood.

When you love one person truly, deeply and sincerely, you can receive love from many people.

When you give your full devotion to one master, you gain your true position.

Even though you had a previous master, a previous method of practice, or a previous lover: do not try comparing them with what you now have. Do not regret the past. Forget the past and offer all of your devotion 100 percent to that one which you now have.

From now on, only go with one. This is the path for fixing your past mistakes, and it is the utmost method for finding your true self and becoming an absolute, correct human being.

166. November 9, 1992. Paris

When the path you are following is clear, all obstacles, blockages and devils disappear. But when the path you are following is not clear, all obstacles, blockages and devils appear.

Then what is the correct path to follow? It is the path of practice.

The path of practice is the path of eliminating one's karma and finding one's true self. This path seems to be very difficult sometimes because you are eliminating karma you created before. But while you are following this correct path, you will have correct relationships, you will get into correct situations, and you will live a correct life. Also, when you are on this path, you will not have any fears. Without fears, you will always live life securely and appreciatively. Living this correct life every day will lead you to the attainment of Buddhahood.

This is like being able, even if you are walking on the darkest of nights, to see the bright light awaiting you somewhere; because you clearly know that it is there, as you walk you are very joyful and satisfied. At the same time, you share this joy with others, make them fulfilled, and your footsteps are very light. La, la, la!!!

167. November 10, 1992. Paris

The world that we see through the eyes is the dark world.
The world that we see through the mind is the bright world.
The world that we see through the eyes is the karma world.
The world that we see through the bright mind is the Buddha world.

When one's mind is bright, one sees Buddha; when one's mind is not bright and clear, one sees sentient beings. Always find your mind lantern and see Buddha. With Buddha eyes see sentient beings and live a correct human being's life.

I want to ask you a *kongan*. The eyes you are seeing with now, are they Buddha eyes or are they sentient being eyes? If you say, "Buddha eyes," that is wrong; and if you say, "sentient being eyes," that is also wrong. What is the correct answer?

168. November 11, 1992. Paris

If you have a lot of conditions and greed, you can easily lose your position because of your conditions, and you can easily lose yourself because of your greed.

People who have a lot of conditions are like those who cannot find their own true light on a dark night. People who have a lot of greed suffer in the dark and are lost and lonely.

When you eliminate your conditions and greed, you can find yourself. When you find yourself and you no longer have conditions and greed, you can get everything you need.

Make the dark night as bright as day and live an unhindered life.

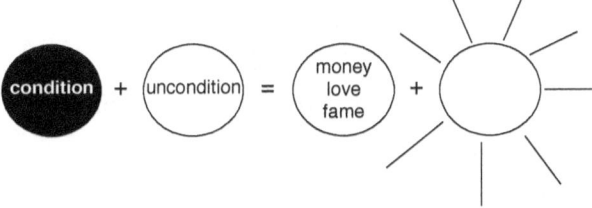

169. November 12, 1992. Paris

In the truth, there is something constantly moving. This is what is called the mind. The mind is not a crooked thing, not a thick or thin thing. It depends on how you use it. That which uses the mind is called thinking. If this thinking is about Buddha, the mind creates Buddha; and if this thinking is about devils, the mind creates devils.

For example, no matter how nice looking a person's form is, if his thinking is ugly, the mind makes this good-looking form ugly; and if this form body is ugly, but the thinking is beautiful, the mind makes the ugly form beautiful.

So always sustain this thinking that uses the mind in a clear way and strive to keep this thinking correct. With this clear thinking, use the mind correctly, without taint and without hindrance, so that you become a completely liberated person. When you become absolutely liberated, you can use the mind which is in the truth however you like.

170. November 13, 1992. Paris

Perceive from where your emotions, feelings, judgments and expressions that are passing through the six gates (eyes, ears, nose, tongue, skin and mind) are coming. Are they coming from the conditioned or from the unconditioned?

If they are coming from the conditioned, they are coming from karma. But if they are coming from the unconditioned, they are coming from the clear o.

One always regrets actions proceeding from the conditioned through the six gates, and these actions put oneself into negativity. But actions that proceed from the unconditional through the six gates are free of hindrances and always make oneself bright.

Before you put into action what comes through the six gates, always perceive yourself. Are your actions coming from conditions or from the unconditioned?

If you cannot distinguish whether it is coming from conditions or the absence of conditions, refrain from that action, put your thinking in the o, and give time and space to the six gates. This is conducting yourself prudently, and it is a way for you to receive respect from others. This is the path of Buddha.

171. November 14, 1992. Monte Carlo

Making the body you now have was a very difficult process:

1. You have to have had good karma in the previous life. This is the cause for being able to make the human body you now have.
2. You have to have had very close relationships with others in the previous life. This is the cause for meeting your parents. If you did not have a close relationship with them, you could not have been born to them.
3. If you do not have a place which you like the most from your last life, you cannot be born.
4. Even after you are born, if you do not have the energy to support the body, you cannot keep it.
5. If you are not with someone you love or are without anyone you gives you love, it is very difficult to keep this body.

This is why you must appreciate all that you have, always make good karma, and give rise to the conviction that you are able to give love to everybody. With that conviction of love, create a loving mind. With that loving mind, you can make a beautiful body eternally and always be born on this beautiful planet.

172. November 15, 1992. Monte Carlo

When you begin practicing, there are many hopes, many expectations, many things to know and many things to do. It is full of wishes.

When your practice is already established and you are in the midst of it, there are many difficulties, there is no way to accomplish what you want, your expectations have not yet been fulfilled, and there is a lot of disappointment. Many times a lot of angry mind appears. Sometimes you forget why you are practicing and there are often lots of regrets.

Passing through and transcending this period is very difficult. But as you do, your karma disappears. And as your karma disappears, understanding finally dawns about what practice is really about.

When practice has been fully realized, the wishes, expectations and wanting you might have experienced all disappear. There is nothing to be angry about, and there are no reasons for being disappointed.

What remains is: when there is sadness, becoming sad; when there is happiness, becoming happy; when there is satisfaction, becoming satisfied. But then you do not know where you are; you do not know what you are. It is just like questioning yourself: "Who am I? What am I?"

Always put all your effort and questions about "What am I?" into everyday life. Just keep on practicing and do your best 100 percent in the midst of daily life. Simply do this every day. Then suddenly, while eating breakfast, become enlightened; while working, become enlightened; while looking at the stars in the sky, become enlightened.

173. November 16, 1992. Monte Carlo

To become a Buddha is very difficult. After becoming a Buddha, living a Buddha's life is very easy; but to live a sentient being's life is very difficult.

A sentient being's life is like a spider web. To free yourself from there is to become a Buddha and live always in a bright and comfortable place. That is why going back into the spider web of a sentient beings' life is very difficult.

In order to teach sentient beings, you touch and feel one spider web string at a time. Giving this one-string-at-a time teaching to sentient beings is very difficult. This way of teaching is Social Buddhism—a live teaching and great bodhisattva action.

This way of teaching, case by case, moment by moment, is very difficult; but this difficult job is very interesting and through it you come to feel and appreciate the living, present form much more widely and deeply.

174. November 17, 1992. Monte Carlo

When you master the method of using the mind, becoming a Buddha is very easy. After you become a Buddha, even while living in the social world you can live an untainted life, and through that untainted and bright life you can help all sentient beings.

This method of using the mind is, for example: if you are in a noisy street, you put yourself into the beautiful *samadhi* and are not bothered by the noise; if you are in a situation in which you normally would become angry and humiliated, you put yourself into the bright o and all anger and humiliation disappear.

How you use your mind is very important. Practice vigorously and become a master of using the mind method.

Being a correct master of the mind is not hearing, speaking or looking at the six gates, but rather hearing, speaking and looking at what is beyond the six gates in the 0, thus having your choice of where you put your mind in each situation, moment by moment.

175. November 18, 1992. Monte Carlo

Whoever knows how to do *samadhi* very well knows very well how to use the method of the mind.

Whoever knows how to do *samadhi* very well does not have any hindrances or obstacles in his mind.

The mind which does *samadhi* is the mind which does not have ego, arrogance or self-protection. This is completely clear and free mind.

Using this completely bright and clear mind freely means going beyond good and bad, beyond right and wrong. This is uncalculating mind. The free mind's brilliance and clarity allow you to make everybody happy and give love to everybody. Because you can give love to everybody, this mind is already 'become-Buddha' mind.

Do not become discouraged because you cannot do *samadhi* very well. Before you do *samadhi*, remove your conditions, ego and self-protections which tie you up. Especially those who have a lot of conditions should first find out what kind of conditions they have gotten caught by and take these off, one by one.

I put myself into the wide, blue ocean, wash away all of my obstacles and conditions in the waves, becoming one with the ocean and flowing freely. This ocean is me, I am this ocean.

Svlong, svlong, swooshhhhh…

176. November 19, 1992. Paris

There is a thing which always turns nothingness into somethingness. Buddha and sentient beings have this thing.

When there is something, Buddha uses this thing to turn something into nothing, and also generates beautiful, great compassion and great love.

But when there is nothing, sentient beings use this thing to turn nothing into something and become slaves to this something which they made themselves. That something becomes a rope with which they tie and bind themselves, and then they suffer, not knowing how to get free from it.

Find this thing which sometimes turns nothing into something and sometimes turns something into nothing. Leave behind that something which you have made; become like a Buddha and have the taste of true nothingness.

P. S. This is a special teaching for people who have been practicing for many years.

177. November 20, 1992. Paris

Before flowers bloom, they suffer from the wind and rain. But one morning, without warning, the flowers bloom and butterflies and bees swarm around them. All darkness disappears where those beautiful open flowers are; it is peaceful and beautiful.

People who practice have a very difficult time while they are doing their practice. But then one morning, they attain enlightenment. They then receive much respect from others, and with this true beauty and peacefulness they can help others.

Even while they remain in the quiescent place, they are helping others. Their mere presence is helping others; when they are just sitting they are helping others; and while going about their normal activities they are helping others. Also, other people only have to think about the enlightened person to receive help.

Wherever the enlightened person goes, darkness disappears and becomes bright and that brightness illuminates sentient beings' 84,000 delusions.

178. November 21, 1992. Paris

Always think within the bright clear o and do not follow the 84,000 thoughts.

To eliminate those 84,000 thoughts, first think about o. When o is clear, put beautiful thinking in there. This thinking leads you into the path of happiness and into having true, great love.

Beautiful thinking is not placing conditions and not placing judgments. That thinking is "before thinking." Find this "before thinking" through practice.

179. November 22, 1992. Paris

One morning, from the 0, 84,000 bodhisattvas come down into this *saha* world:

Eliminate 84,000 delusions. Do 84,000 bodhisattva actions.

84,000 devils simultaneously become Buddha. 84,000 brilliant lights shine, eliminating this *saha* world.

Suddenly one morning, this world becomes an absolute Buddha world, adorned with 84,000 true beauties and this shining makes 84,000,000,000 (84 billion) sentient beings happy.

180. November 23, 1992. Paris

Whoever can help others is the already clear.

Whoever can be a true secretary for others is already clear. The way of truly helping others is: first, eliminate one's conditions; second, always respect other's conditions; and third, *always meet other people's needs.*

To be a person who can really help others: *Do not try to be a boss for others, be their truthful secretary.*

Being a truthful secretary always makes you shine. This is true bodhisattva action and is the path of Buddha.

181. November 23, 1992. Paris

Do not only hope for comfort. Being busy as a bee: this is the true, alive life.

When you have a being-busy-as-a-bee life: this is a good time. When you have nothing to do: that is a tasteless life.

When you have a taste of the good and bad things, and you are busy as a bee: that is a youthful life. When there is nothing left to taste: that is the end of the life.

So do not be afraid of a life being busy as a bee, and be happy when you are in a being-busy-as-a-bee life.

182. November 23, 1992. In flight from Paris to Los Angeles

I make myself a Buddha.

I make myself a bodhisattva.

I make myself a devil.

With a beautiful smile and soft, sympathetic speech, I make myself a Buddha.

"How may I help you?" This sentence makes me a bodhisattva.

When I cannot conquer my emotions and conditions, this angry countenance makes me a devil.

This 'I', no matter how much you try, is very difficult to find. Also, this 'I' makes me become all kinds of different levels (Buddha, bodhisattva, devil).

So before you try finding this 'I': first practice to become a Buddha and a bodhisattva. The day you become a Buddha and a bodhisattva: ask that Buddha and bodhisattva what this 'I' is.

183. November 24, 1992. Los Angeles

Do not trust only what you hear and see. Do not follow other people's actions.

In this world, there are many things that are confusing. Before you follow what you hear and see, first look into yourself. Is an action helping or hindering your path of practice? If it is helping your path of practice, then you may continue.

If you only follow other people's actions, you are following other people's karma. Do not make unnecessary karma and suffering for yourself.

The tongue has no bone. That is correct. But human beings should make a bone with their vow and practice and be able to watch themselves.

184. November 25, 1992. Honolulu
Stop that thinking which aims at showing off.

Before you try showing off, think of what will make others comfortable. Before you try showing off, think of what will make everyone comfortable.

This great thinking already touches others' minds and eyes. With this thinking, you automatically receive love and respect from others.

Show off thinking lowers oneself. Thinking about others is thinking that shows oneself correctly. This correct display of thinking leads to finding the correct Buddha path.

185. November 26, 1992. Honolulu
Every human being is the same, but because of individual karma they use the energy (of practice, of the universe) in all different ways. People who have lighter karma receive love and respect from others and make the energy comfortable for them. Those who have heavier karma, no matter how intelligent and sincerely correct they

seem to be, make energy that bothers others and cannot receive other's love and respect.

Some people, by their outside form, look very comfortable to deal with; but when you deal with them, it bothers you and ruins your life. Some people, by their outside form, look very difficult to deal with; but when you do so, it does not hinder you and, in fact, in the long run it helps you. You appreciate that person who comforts and who does not bother you.

Through your practice, please become a comfortable person for others, without hindering or bothering them.

186. November 27, 1992. Honolulu

When you get up in the morning, all kinds of various thoughts appear. Of those thoughts, 90 percent come from the 84,000 delusions; 7 percent come from your actions or your present life's karma; and 3 percent are clear perceptions of the following twenty-four hours, until you get up again the next morning.

A clear person always tries to eliminate 97 percent of those thoughts and tries to keep the remaining 3 percent, all day long. An unclear person gets caught by the 97 percent of his or her thinking, forgets about the other 3 percent, loses himself or herself, and does not know how and what to do all day long.

Even though those who are clear also have to deal with that 97 percent, they can take it as a pleasure which is coming from this present form, and can still keep the 3 percent very strongly. But those who are unclear suffer from this 97 percent and loses the 3 percent.

187. November 28, 1992. Honolulu

People look at others according to their individual karma. That is why people have different opinions when they see the Buddha.

How you look at the Buddha is what makes oneself. When you look at the Buddha very respectfully and gloriously, that vision makes you a respectful and glorious human being. But when you look at the Buddha disrespectfully and disdainfully, you become a disrespectful and disdainful human being.

It is the same with masters and with partners. When you respect your master and follow the teachings, you receive respect from others and can be a leader and teacher. Also, when you respect and love your partner, you become a person who receives respect and love from your partner.

In this world of opposites, make your own appreciative and shining world. This is the one great method to rip through the spider's web.

188. November 29, 1992. Honolulu

The person who knows what his or her mistake is and tries to fix it is on the Buddha path. The person who knows what his or her mistake is, but does not want to fix it and only insists upon his opinion, is far away from the Buddha path.

Those who insist on their opinions and who try to cover up their mistakes do so because they have a lot of deficiencies. But rather than having deficiencies, whoever tries to fix his or her mistakes has a lot of ambition and liveliness. That ambition is to make one's own creations, and it is connected to supernatural, penetration power. It is because of Buddha's ambition, which is great love and compassion, that human beings are created from the o.

Those on the Buddha path have far greater ambition than those who are not.

189. November 30, 1992. Honolulu

1. There seem to be many headaches while living this life.
2. If you think about things one by one, nothing seems to please your mind.
3. You try to do everything correctly, but they do not work out that way and so everything seems to be uncomfortable and you have many annoyances.

But look at it this way:

1. Take the headaches as your teachers.
2. Take as a Buddha that which seems not to please your mind.
3. When you try to do things correctly but they do not work out that way, take that as your vigorous practice.

When you conduct yourself this way:

1. That which gives you a headache turns you into a leader.
2. That mind which seems not to be pleased becomes Buddha mind.
3. All of your annoyances turn you into a bodhisattva and enable you to do bodhisattva action.

190. December 1, 1992. Honolulu

Preview of the Month

This is the month of love. Open up everything which built-up and became knotted inside of you during the past eleven months and let love inside.

Enjoy this love as much as you can. Love without condition. Relax. Be happy.

191. December 1, 1992. Honolulu

When Buddha looks at sentient beings he always gives a smile of love and compassion. The reason is that when sentient beings do things, sometimes their actions seem to be so ignorant and sometimes that's so cute. In some small matter, they think that they are the best and broadcast their righteousness. And when things go wrong, they make a big scene and complain about it.

All of these things seem to be so interesting and yet so pitiable. But no matter what sentient beings do, Buddha always looks at everything with a love mind.

If sentient beings' minds are connected even one inch to the Buddha mind, they can really live a comfortable and happy life.

192. December 2, 1992. Honolulu

While you are practicing, no matter what kind of situations appear in front of you, do not be afraid.

We human beings have a lot of knowledge and experience and we hear many things. In other words, we have a lot of information in our heads and so it's difficult to get away from the world of opposites.

When you look at things and situations, at first you do so from the negative point of view. At the same time, you try not to go into negativity, but you do even so.

So practice person: if you do not want to go into negativity, no matter what things and situations appear, always be willing to take a risk and do not think that you may regret it. Look at whatever situation appears in front of you without thinking about being successful or regretful about it. Just do it. When you just do it, at that time you can find yourself and you will know yourself much more clearly.

Remember: we human beings come to this sentient beings' world to have all kinds of experiences, tastes and sights. That is why we are here. Also, remember that in the other worlds there is nothing to do; they are very boring.

193. December 3, 1992. Honolulu

When someone is happy and has a happy situation, congratulate him as much as you can. And when another person has a happy situation and you do not have one of your own, do not be jealous or pessimistic about it. Your pessimism and jealousy will enchain you and that chain will block your good and happy situation from coming.

So when someone has a happy situation, open your heart and congratulate him truly and honestly. That congratulatory mind is our true self's mind.

That congratulatory mind will come back to you, and then you will have a happy situation like others do. The quantity of your sincere congratulations is matched by the quantity of happiness that will come back to you.

Remember: when you give others 1, you receive 2; and when you give others -1, you receive -3.

$$0 + 1 = 2$$
$$0 - 1 = -3$$

194. December 4, 1992. Honolulu

As the earth turns beneath the sun and moon, they always see what is going on here. No matter what appears, the sun and moon do not discriminate about it and only quiescently see what occurs.

No matter what kind of bad situation appears, they never scold anyone. But when it is very bad, they will act angrily, making thunder and lightning and giving love and compassion rains to make people realize what they have been doing. When good things happen, the sun and moon shine brilliantly, making the whole world bright. Always, without ever once turning away, leaving or deceiving the world, they watch it turn.

This form body, while seeing the revolving earth for 45 years has seen and heard many things. But as time passes, all expectations, disappointments and angry mind are disappearing, and, at the same time, this form can see that sentient beings are lovelier and cuter than before. Its only thinking is about how to alleviate sentient beings' suffering and make them happier. This thinking is getting stronger and stronger than ever before.

How many more revolutions will it take to fulfill their wishes?

195. December 5, 1992. Honolulu

Wherever you go, whatever you hear, whatever you see, do not be a monkey. Become a master of the monkey and regardless of what may be too little or too much for the monkey, catch and tame the monkey and become its parents.

Become a friend of the monkey. Lead this monkey to the path of Buddha, and the day you become a Buddha, become a Buddha together with the monkey.

196. December 6, 1992. Honolulu

Buddha is in front of your eyes, but you cannot see Buddha because you are thinking of 'Buddha' through your own karma. This makes the day of becoming a Buddha far away.

As your practice deepens, your thinking lessens continuously and it seems that you are becoming stupid. At that time, you can see the Buddha right in front of you and *afterwards, you can live comfortably in Buddha's arms.*

One day, someone suddenly calls out, "Hello, Buddha!" Without thinking, you answer: "Yes!"

197. December 7, 1992. Honolulu

1. Always be a good person.
2. Always be a comfortable person.
3. Always be an understanding person.

1. Make yourself into a good person.
2. Make yourself into a comfortable person.

3. Make yourself into an understanding person.

1. Deal with others as a good person.
2. Deal with others comfortably.
3. Deal with others with understanding.

Forgive everything.
Only remember that the sun is round, the moon is round, and the world is also round.

198. December 8, 1992. Honolulu
Something special.
Very, very special.

199. December 9, 1992. Honolulu
If you want to be successful and have a happy and beautiful life, always strive to do your best in everything. A beautiful life does not come from laziness; it comes from striving to do your best in everything.

In striving, there is a vigorous practice. The end result of striving is becoming a Buddha. *After becoming a Buddha, strive to save all sentient beings. This is the correct function of Buddhahood.*

For the practice person:
1. Strive to eliminate your own karma.
2. While karma is being eliminated, strive to make yourself beautiful.
3. Strive to make others happy.

200. December 10, 1992. Honolulu

Always chasing various kinds of thinking and coming back to yourself.

Regular human beings spend 3 minutes chasing various kinds of thinking, and 3 seconds coming back to themselves. Even those 3 seconds of coming back to themselves, they use very negatively.

Practice people spend 3 minutes chasing various kinds of thinking, and 6 seconds coming back to themselves. They use those 6 seconds of coming back to themselves to eliminate their karma.

Buddha spends 3 seconds chasing various kinds of thinking, and 3 minutes coming back to himself. But he uses those 3 seconds of chasing various kinds of thinking to discover methods for helping sentient beings, and those 3 minutes of returning to himself he gives back to sentient beings and has nothing left.

$3 + 180 = 183 - 180 = 3$

3 is: *Na Mu Kwan Se Um Bo Sal*
Na Mu So Ga Mo Ni Bul
Chong Gak Mio Poep Yon Hwa Kyong

201. December 11, 1992. Honolulu

When problems or agonies appear, do not get caught by them and lose yourself.

Just because of a problem or agony, do not deviate from your daily schedule. Observe your regular daily schedule, hang the problem or agony on the outside of the door, and as you come and go, look at it once in a while.

Then, when you suddenly have an exquisite idea, go outside and look at your problem or agony again. *The problem or agony that was hanging on the door has disappeared, and only the string that it was hanging from is still there, dangling in the wind.*

A couple of days later, go outside and have another look. Even the string will have disappeared; the warm sun is shining brightly and one's smiling face becomes round.

202. December 12, 1992. Honolulu

Do 370 prostrations without stopping.
Sit down. Breathe in and out 7 times.
Repeat the mantra 300 times.
Perceive what kind of thinking appears at that moment.

203. December 13, 1992. Honolulu

Buddha means nothing.
Sentient being means something.
Something always depends on nothing.
Nothing depends on something and shines.
Nothing and something are not separate; they always exist together.

Depending on nothing (Buddha) will make you beautiful. To make yourself beautiful, first throw away your small I (desires, conditions and opinions expressing karma) and find nothing, which means Buddha. This is the practice.

When you find that nothing which is Buddha, you can get everything.

When you follow something, you can lose everything.

204. December 14, 1992. Honolulu

Buddha's supernatural penetration power is incalculable. Human thinking cannot even imagine what this power is. This power creates everything; it creates the universe and human beings.

When you use this power which creates everything beautifully, this whole world becomes beautiful. How can this power be connected to human beings? Connection to this power comes from the mind. When the mind is clean and clear, you are connected to this power; when the mind is not clear, you are never connected with it.

To make a clean and clear mind, first you must keep your thinking beautiful. Always keep beautiful thinking and eliminate whichever hindrances arise in the mind. Then you will connect to this power, you will become a master of the power, and you will be an absolutely free person.

Become a master of this supernatural penetration power and teach others how to also become masters of it.

205. December 15, 1992. Honolulu

Beautiful thinking comes from a thankful mind.

1. Thankful to the Buddha for making you come into this world.
2. Thankful to your parents for giving birth and raising you.
3. Thankful to the master for eliminating your darkness and opening up wisdom for you.
4. Thankful to your husband or wife for giving you love and full security.

5. Thankful to everybody for approving that you are alive.
This thankful mind is the one which makes beautiful thinking.

206. December 16, 1992. Wailea, Maui

Human beings come from the place of nothing. But being a human being means to be something. This is the reason human beings are attached to something, because of which they suffer.

When you put down that something, suffering disappears. When you also put down that nothing, you become a Buddha.

If we human beings, with our present human forms, put down both something and nothing and use our forms for others, we will have true happiness and appreciation of being alive.

207. December 17, 1992. Wailea, Maui

Do not complain about or criticize others.

Before you complain about or criticize others, first look into yourself. Complaining about and criticizing others is like making a scar in the o.

When complaints and criticism appear, cover them with love. With true love, help fix the situation, putting down the thinking that you want to fix others. If you really want to fix another's mistake, just respect and love them unconditionally.

Remember, in true love everything becomes beautiful as time goes by. This is the way of complete harmony and contentment.

208. December 18, 1992. Wailea, Maui

Laziness means losing yourself. Laziness is to separate from others, to go into the path of loneliness, and to make yourself poor.

When someone needs or depends on you, do not be lazy; do your best. Doing your best for others is your great opportunity to eliminate your bad karma and reinforce your good karma. This good karma will be your great asset; using it, you can live richly and happily in this life, and life after life.

When a person is not rich in this life, it means that he or she was lazy and did not help others sincerely in his last life.

209. December 19, 1992. Wailea, Maui

Human beings' original mind is beautiful. But because of being born here in this form, and because of having to survive, you attach to life and make karma. You then attach to that karma, and because of that you lose your beautiful mind and suffer.

So find the mind which is before birth and before making karma. *To do this, keep thinking that human beings' original mind is beautiful.* With that thinking, keep that beautiful human beings' original mind.

210. December 20, 1992. Honolulu

Today's energy is not comfortable. So, be careful about your speech, action and thinking.

Today, forget about yourself. Only think about making others happy, unconditionally.

211. December 21, 1992. Honolulu

Our karma is just like a coconut shell. But in that shell there is clear water which is just like our true nature. So, how can you eliminate that karma which is hard like a coconut shell? To eliminate it is not to break the shell. All you have to do is make a hole in it and let the water come out.

It is the same thing with karma. Eliminating karma does not mean throwing it away. Polish your karma like a shell that you have come out of. Look at it once in a while and show others how to polish their own shells.

Practice means making a hole in the coconut shell.

212. December 22, 1992. Honolulu

Do not think about anything.
Do not be hindered by anything.
Do not miss anything.
When you look at the sky, just see the sky.
When you look at the earth, just see the earth.
When you can count the stars in the sky one by one, that
    is true tranquility and clarity.
One star, one I; two stars, two I; three stars, three I.

213. December 23, 1992. Honolulu

Become a master of the mind.
Become a master of thinking.

When you become a slave to thinking, you lose the master of the mind. When you lose the master of the mind, you become a slave to karma.

In this moment, put whatever thinking you have into the o, concentrate, and see that the wall is white, the carpet is red. Also, believe that master, that "something" which sees the wall is white, the carpet is red.

Believe that master.

214. December 24, 1992. Honolulu

Do not try to show off what you are.
Make your best effort in whatever you do.
Showing yourself off is cutting yourself off.
Without showing off, when you put all of your effort into your work, that is the path of building up your own virtue.

215. December 24, 1992. Honolulu

Even if you are clear and bright, if someone irritates you, that irritation makes you angry; and because of that anger, you lose your patience. Also, because of that angry thinking you lose the whole day, you lose the virtue that you have built up until now, and you slide back again into the suffering world.

So, when there is an angry situation and angry thinking, immediately think about the o; go outside and bury that angry situation and thinking in the ground. Then repeat the mantra three times and *hapchang* three times to the Buddha.

216. December 25, 1992. Honolulu

When you help others out of attachment and desire, it will bring great disappointment and sadness in the future.

When without attachment and desire you just help others according to the relationships and situations you share, though these will not shine immediately, they will do so as time goes by.

So today, no matter what situations appear and no matter who you meet or do not meet, do your best in your duties. That is truly helping others without attachment or desire.

217. December 25, 1992. Honolulu

When a wise person jokes, it always makes others happy and gives them great teaching.

When an unwise person jokes, it hurts others' feelings and makes them suffer. And, the same amount of suffering will come back to this person in the future.

A joke comes from a truth. Unclear truth creates the joke.

P. S. No one is a holy or unholy person from birth. It is only your speech and actions which make you holy or unholy.

218. December 26, 1992. Honolulu

The ripe fruit never has any conditions, never yearns for anything, and only emits a beautiful fragrance. It hangs on the tree, waiting for someone to pick and eat it; and when someone does eat it, that fruit's duty is finished and whoever ate it becomes happy.

But the unripe fruit is always waiting for rain to come and for the sun to shine, and wants to have good weather all of the time.

It hangs on the tree and tries to prevent anyone from picking and eating it. Because of its fear of being picked and eaten, it is prone to becoming angry and if anyone does pick and eat that fruit, they suffer.

See yourself. Are you a ripe or an unripe fruit? Check yourself at least once a day.

219. December 27, 1992. Honolulu

We human beings are living inside of love, but we do not know that. Only when our conditions and desires are disappearing do we finally realize, little by little, that we are living inside of love.

But no matter how many conditions and desires we have, when we *remember and realize that we are living inside of love* we will not get caught by them. We will use these conditions and desires correctly, to live a truthful life.

The conditions and desires which know love are Buddha's conditions and desires. But the conditions and desires which do not know love are human beings' conditions and desires.

220. December 28, 1992. Honolulu

Looking at the sky and the earth, we cannot grasp their size. Because we are exhausted from living, our mind has become very narrow.

That exhausted mind disappears, however, when we really see the sky and the earth. At that moment, we realize that what had been exhausted was nothing but our form. Realizing this, we can fix our exhausted form. Then, we can determine which conditions and desires coming through the six gates we should eliminate and which ones to keep, and we can start a new, happy life.

221. December 29, 1992. Honolulu

No matter how much you try saying correct words to strongly opinionated people, they do not want to believe you. Also, if these strongly opinionated people do not get what they want, they become very disappointed and feel as though they have lost everything.

So before you become disappointed by your own opinion, check first to see if it is correct or not. At that time, you can truly realize how ignorant you have been, and through your strong disappointment you can find your new self again.

A strongly opinionated person wakes up the holy person from his sleep, becomes the unholy person's boss and makes many people suffer.

222. December 30, 1992. Honolulu

Find the interest when there is no interest.
Find the usage when there is no usage.
Find the taste when there is no taste.

When you can do that, you can find your true I. This way you can graciously keep that true I without wrinkling and breaking it. At the same time, you can protect and keep this I and can protect and help others.

223. December 31, 1992. Honolulu

The earth revolves around the sun, starting from one point and coming back to the same point. The moon revolves around the earth, starting from one point and coming back to the same point.

Human thinking is the same. It starts from one point, goes around and comes back to the same point. No matter what kind of thinking appears, the point of return is the same as the beginning point. But while your thinking goes around it is either *yang* or *yin*, and according to this your life shifts and changes.

When thinking is *yang*, life becomes *yang*; when thinking is *yin*, life becomes *yin*. But whether it is *yang* or *yin*, the starting point is the same. *When thinking completely disappears, that original starting point also disappears.*

If you understand this, you can become a master of your thinking, and at the same time you can find your absolute, true self and will be able to create whatever kind of life you want, without depending on anybody.

P. S. Read this teaching 300 times.

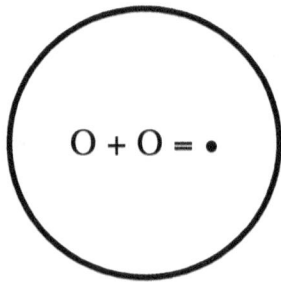

www.ingramcontent.com/pod-product-compliance
Lightning Source LLC
Chambersburg PA
CBHW022013160426
43197CB00007B/408